Group Games

Early Speech & Language Skills

A sensorimotor approach

Titles in the Group Games Series

Group Games

Early Speech & Language Skills

A sensorimotor approach

MARIA MONSCHEIN

Speechmark

DEDICATION

These games are primarily dedicated to children with speech and language difficulties and their parents.

Originally published in German by Don Bosco Verlag, München under the title *Spiele zur Sprach-förderung, Band 1 & 2*, © Don Bosco Verlag, München 1997, 1998

Published in 2006 by
Speechmark Publishing Ltd, Telford Road, Bicester, Oxon OX26 4LQ, UK
Telephone +44 (0)1869 244644   Facsimile +44 (0)1869 320040
www.speechmark.net

002-5269/Printed in the United Kingdom/1010

British Library Cataloguing in Publication Data

Monschein, Maria
   Early speech & language skills. – (Group Games) (A Speechmark practical activity resource)
   1. Group play therapy 2. Recreational therapy for children
   3. Speech therapy for children – Exercises
   I. Title
   618.9'2891653

ISBN-10: 0 86388 543 8
ISBN-13: 978 0 86388 543 3

Contents

About the Author

Maria Monschein is a language teacher and runs a private school for the holistic development of language promotion. She is based in Austria.

Acknowledgements

I would like to say a special and heartfelt thank you to my daughters, Stefanie and Miriam, who participated in the games with joy and lots of eagerness. A big thank you also to my husband Fred, who was always there to help me with good advice and gave me the courage to write this book.

Thank you to Lilo Seelos, the translator.

Note: For the purposes of clarity alone, the group facilitator is referred to as 'she' and the group member is referred to as 'he'.

List of Games

Games for developing visual skills and hand-eye coordination 308

Introduction

This book is intended for everyone who is interested in promoting the speech and language development of children aged 3–11 years. Educators, teachers, specialist language teachers, speech & language therapists, parents and childminders will find that the games are fun, encourage imagination and aim to develop a child's whole personality.

All of the games are suitable for children experiencing difficulties with either the articulation of speech sounds and sound sequences or with the grammar and production of whole sentences, as well as for children whose language development is delayed. While playing the games, children who are experiencing difficulties with the production of continuous speech become absorbed in what they are doing and are distracted from the conscious act of talking. As the games are successfully played, so their self-esteem grows and their speech and language improves. Of course, these games can also be played with children who have no specific speech and language difficulties.

I would encourage any parents reading this book to play these games with their children; it will help their children's speech and language and their overall development. However, if parents are in any way concerned about their child's speech and language development, I would advise them to seek advice from a qualified speech & language therapist who will be able to assess the child and put together a specific and individualised programme of activities. The only requirement is that your child is enjoying the games. If a child does not like a specific game or exercise, I would advise you against trying to convince or even force the child to participate in the exercises.

The main rationale behind all the games is that speech and language development is closely linked to all senses working together. Speech, language, and motor development are neurophysiologically linked.

Language is only possible if the brain is able to interpret and integrate effectively the different sensory stimuli. All sensations that flow to the brain via the different senses – around the head (ears, eyes, nose, mouth) as well as any other part of the body (muscles, joints, vital organs, the tiniest areas of skin) – need to be organised in such a way that we can respond accordingly, planning and executing motor movements, learning and understanding and finally producing spoken language (Ayres AJ, 1984, 1992, *Milestones in Child Development*, Springer, Berlin, Heidelberg, New York).

However, because children's sensory development is often delayed, or because there are some children who require a higher than normal degree of sensory stimulation, speech and language facilitation should always start with, or be combined with, a basic general facilitation of the senses. It is particularly important that the three primary sensory systems – the tactile, proprioceptive and vestibular senses – receive sufficient stimulation. Only when these three basic senses are functioning appropriately is it possible to work on developing other skills. They are the foundation. Each game should therefore aim to appeal to as many senses as possible, so that many different stimuli are perceived and integrated. As a result, new links and connections are made in the brain and the child's capacity to learn grows.

We know that language is the most important foundation for building interpersonal relationships. *The best language facilitation is a good and intensive relationship with the child.* All three of the primary sensory systems mentioned above are stimulated through the mother's movement when the child is still in the womb. Only with plenty of affection and love from adults, as well as recognition and attention to the interests and needs of the child in his first years, can these sensory systems continue to develop in a meaningful and effective manner. Language development is facilitated when parents interact well with the child, accepting him for who he is, as well as asking questions and showing interest in his play.

The way in which parents deal with children's questions during the so-called 'questions phase' (around the ages of three and four) also represents a decisive factor for a child's language development. If children are not encouraged to ask questions but are ignored or receive thoughtless and reluctant answers to their questions, they learn not to ask any more questions. Instead, they learn to accept objects and situations whose names and purpose they do not understand, and which therefore can not be integrated into their conceptual knowledge (Schenk-Danziger L, 1993, *Developmental Psychology*, ÖBV Pädagogischer Verlag, Vienna).

A lack of interest in and affection for the child may also mean that he is unable to develop his senses in an age-appropriate way. Essentially, he does not receive enough input for his brain to lay down the necessary pathways. If a child finds himself in an environment where there are limited possibilities for stimulating the tactile sense (the ability to perceive touch), or where he is not encouraged to explore things through touch, he is likely to have problems with his conceptual development and understanding. A child needs to encounter a concept in many different contexts before he is able to generalise freely and apply that concept. For example, in order to be able to apply the abstract concept of 'soft', a child needs to experience both 'hard' and 'soft' (such as skin, cotton wool, fur, hair, feathers, duvets) objects.

The proprioceptive sense (perception of stimuli received through muscles, ligaments and joints) and the vestibular sense (sense of balance) can only be developed through sufficient movement. However, as more children are increasingly moving less, they are in danger of being deprived of essential stimuli. Most families now have at least one car, and it is becoming increasingly unusual to walk anywhere. Many children live in small flats or play in structured playgrounds, or sit in front of the television for hours on end without moving. By doing these things they gain few sensory experiences. In addition, today's emphasis on academic achievement may lead parents and nursery teachers to offer children educational games and worksheets instead of movement games or the chance to explore the natural world. Both of these would provide children with more varied and diverse experiences, and therefore much more plentiful stimulation for the brain.

It is the child's whole personality that needs to be appealed to and whose development should be facilitated. Children enjoy movement and want to use all their senses and let their imagination go. Imagination is a fundamental and important issue for children in today's world. Who actually still has the time to encourage and listen to children's imaginary stories? Parents often need to go back to work full-time just as their children's imagination begins to blossom, and may not feel like listening to the imaginary stories of their children, much less joining in and letting their own imagination flow.

Unfortunately, in today's society, children's daily routines are sometimes as proscribed as those of many adults. This does not leave children with much opportunity to engage either in free play or to structure their own time. Even some nurseries now run tightly packed programmes which leave younger children with less of an opportunity for free play and imaginary thinking. When working with children, I have often noticed how much they can be engaged in play, and how they can be led to attempt exercises again and again when these are incorporated into imaginary stories. The contribution of the adult's imagination and creativity is invaluable. Children will show great enthusiasm for such 'imaginary journeys' and will bring their own powerfully creative imaginations to their play.

How to Use the Games

The exercises and games in this book are designed to facilitate brain development and therefore the development of personality. All the activities aim to involve the child's entire body and thus offer plenty of 'foundation training' for the brain. The exercises concentrate on the development of functions which involve proprioceptive, vestibular and tactile sensations because these three sensory systems are of fundamental importance for speech and language development. An improved body awareness and sensory integration of vestibular, tactile, auditory and visual senses will enable the development and strengthening of the child's motor coordination, agility, dexterity, speed of reaction, emotional stability and, of course, language skills.

WHAT EQUIPMENT IS NEEDED?
The games require few resources, but standard gym equipment (such as skipping ropes, rhythmic bands, hoops, balls, beanbags, rope ladders, skateboard, trampoline, hammock, swing, stilts, gym mats and similar items) is used repeatedly. Equipment which requires children to adjust their movement against gravity is of particular importance, because many children with speech and language difficulties also have motor difficulties, particularly with regard to their balance system (vestibular area).

Some of the activities require some basic art and craft materials (particularly natural materials, clay, play dough – for recipe, see Game 244, *Play dough*, page 298 – paper, fabric, wool, beads, corks, wooden and polystyrene balls) which can enable group creativity. Such group work provides opportunities for developing the children's fine motor skills. Most of the time children will get great enjoyment out of the things they have created and will be proud of their achievements. It is essential that the children are really allowed to do things themselves, such as using scissors or a particular tool, or having the chance to do some painting and drawing.

It is particularly important that all of the children practise at an active rather than symbolic level (the latter, unfortunately, is so often the case). They should be fully involved in the exercises, because children are most likely to learn when they are allowed to do and experience things for themselves. This is why the book suggests using real-life objects from the immediate environment, as well as household objects and toys, when playing the games.

One of the main priorities when choosing materials is that the children are allowed to develop their imagination, and handle the materials without having to worry about breaking them. Wooden blocks are particularly well suited for this, as they can represent many things in a child's imagination: houses, towers, cars, trains, bottles, food, glasses, islands, bridges, roads, rail tracks, river banks, magic books, different tools, figures, people, animals, furniture and many other objects.

If we use prefabricated toys, we actually block children's ability to use their imagination and find their own imaginary world, putting them in a position where they will be less able to bring themselves into the game. Through the use of 'raw materials' they may conjure up things that we have not thought to offer them in the first place. Natural materials (such as stones, sticks, fir cones, acorns, conkers, roots, and so on) are also useful.

Some games utilise a 'feely' box (or a 'feely' bag). This is a box covered with a cloth, so the children cannot see the objects inside and have to guess the contents by feeling them. This process particularly develops the child's sense of touch. Picture cards or composite pictures are used as visual aids and for consolidating and practising sounds or sentence structures. Pairs games, lottos, jigsaws, picture stories and similar materials are used in the same way.

HOW THE GAMES ARE STRUCTURED

It is important to remember that children with speech and language difficulties particularly benefit from multi-sensory stimulation. Language is not simply learned through copying, practice and repetition. Rather, those experiences that provide multi-sensory input as foundation training for the brain, and which themselves require to be verbalised, can be the most valuable. Therefore the games often start with a story or incorporate storytelling, providing a basic framework within which different areas can be worked on. The child virtually talks on his own within the framework, on his own initiative. As a result, the language used is closer to natural, spontaneous language than the artificial practice language used during structured table-top therapy activities in front of the mirror. This also takes into consideration that most children will still be at a level of 'magical thinking'. They live in an imaginary world of witches, fairies and magicians. Using games that utilise this imaginary world, the child is given an additional opportunity to work through and develop his creative thinking. The main priority has to be to teach a child to enjoy talking, and this is easily achieved with the help of such story frameworks. In this way we can make joint plans with a child, practise magic spells and talk about routes, means of transport and many other things.

When 'an adult' is mentioned in the text from now on, this refers to the person working, or rather playing, with the child. This can be a specialist language teacher, a speech & language therapist, a class teacher, a carer, a mother, a father, and so on.

WHO ARE THE GAMES FOR?

The exercises are suitable for individual children as well as groups, but for convenience all exercises are described for group use. Most games are suitable for children aged from three to four but will also appeal to older children up to about eleven years. The games are described in an accessible way so that non-professionals can use them without any problems.

The children should be involved in helping with the preparations and set-up for the games, because this provides excellent opportunities for training gross and fine motor skills, as well as stimulating different senses. Some of the exercises suggest sentence sequences that the children could say. I would suggest that, to start with, the adult undertakes to say these sentences until the children take over spontaneously. At no point should any child be actively prompted to speak; instead allow them to start speaking of their own accord. The aim of all the exercises is for the children to talk with enjoyment and without being forced. If the adult unassumingly provides the children with appropriate language models, it normally does not take long before they begin to take this up. All of the children's ideas should be picked up on and incorporated into the game. However, all the exercises should always be verbalised – even if this is only done by the adult.

If you are not planning to practise a particular speech sound with the children you can use household or any other items from the immediate environment, instead of the proposed materials – simply change the sentence sequences accordingly. Despite the fact that the games are divided up to focus on specific senses and language problems, it is inevitable that most of the game ideas will provide opportunities to train several senses and areas at once. The most important thing is that you identify the areas in which children have difficulties and a need to catch up. With a little imagination, the games listed in this book can easily be changed and extended.

The Games

Part 1: Games for developing a sense of touch and proprioception

Children with speech and language problems are sometimes undersensitive with regard to their sense of touch and their proprioceptive sense. The sense of touch processes sensations that occur through touching skin or mucous membranes in order for us to feel that touch. Proprioception refers to sensory information that, at all points in time, tells our brain when and to what extent our muscles are contracting or extending, and when and to what extent our joints are bending, stretching, or are being pulled or pushed. Proprioception also makes it possible for our brains constantly to register the position of each and every body part, and how each part is moving. Together, both senses contribute fundamentally to a person's body perception and are therefore also very important for speaking.

The following games aim to help improve the senses of touch and proprioception and, as a result, speech and language skills.

Games for developing a sense of touch

Real understanding of a concept involves hands-on experience. If a child is confronted with an environment that offers few opportunities to stimulate their sense of touch, or if a child is not encouraged to touch things at all, he is likely to end up experiencing problems with concept development. There are also some children who require more stimulation than is available during their everyday life.

Each child needs to experience the actuality of a concept in many different situations before he is able to apply that concept freely. For example, in order to be able to use the abstract concept 'soft' correctly, many 'soft' experiences (such as cotton wool, fur, hair, a feather duvet, a towel, and so on) are necessary. In order to internalise as many concepts as possible, a child also needs as many touch experiences as possible.

(1) Who could that be?

Depending on the children's developmental age, a minimum of three children is needed to play this game. Each child in turn is studied and described by the rest of the group.

Then one child closes his eyes. One of the children who has already been described stands in front of him, and now has to be recognised through touch only. Who could it be? The child doing the touching can also try to describe what he is feeling: 'I can feel short hair. I can feel a woolly jumper and trousers. It's you, Andrew!'

Aims: tolerating body contact, developing tactile awareness and perception, visual perception, describing physical appearances, learning each other's names, memory training

Materials: none

(2) Blind touch

The children form a circle. One child is blindfold, and stands in the middle of the circle. The blindfold child is spun around, and then has to try to identify the person in front of him, using his sense of touch (by feeling with his hands). He should also try and describe what he is feeling: 'I can feel a head with long hair. Also, a dress and tights. It is …' The blindfold child is allowed to ask the other child questions, in order to recognise him by voice alone.

Aims: developing tactile awareness and perception, being gentle, enjoying talking, developing acoustic perception

Materials: scarf or blindfold

3) Who is the dragon going to eat?

One child plays the dragon. He stands on one side of the room. All of the other children stand on the opposite side of the room. The dragon calls, 'The dragon is going to eat Julie!' Now the other children have to shout, 'No, you are not going to eat Julie!' and try to protect Julie. For example, they can quickly make a circle around her. If the dragon manages to catch the child, that child turns into the dragon and calls out the name of the person he wants to eat.

Aims: developing tactile perception, dexterity, agility, group spirit, consolidating everybody's names, developing articulation (especially *dr*)

Materials: none

4 Holiday souvenir

The children bring to the group objects that they have collected in the holidays (shells, pebbles, snail shells, roots, fir cones, entrance tickets, souvenirs, postcards) or things that they used frequently during the holidays (snorkel, flippers, goggles, swimming trunks, swimming costume, towels, sun screen, sunglasses, binoculars, camera, map, roller skates, ball, badminton racket). If they want to, the children can also talk about specific holiday experiences.

The objects are then placed under a blanket. Each child has to feel an object and name it. If a child names an object wrongly, or is unable to give it a name, it is put back under the blanket and another child tries to guess a different object. Once all objects have been felt and guessed, they are put back under the blanket. Now the children need to recall what is under the blanket, saying, 'There is a … under the blanket.' If they can remember correctly, they are given the object to hold. The game continues until there is nothing left under the blanket.

Finally, five objects can be lined up and the children can take turns to recall them with their eyes closed. Each child is given his own objects (he could always try and break his own personal record by increasing the number of objects, one at a time). Perhaps the individual objects would also like to talk about what they have experienced. To do this, each child could choose an object and pretend to talk on behalf of the object.

Aims: developing tactile perception, vocabulary, use of preposition *under*, developing memory, visual perception (line perception), imagination

Materials: objects that remind children of holidays, blanket

5 Vegetable harvest

Different vegetables are put on the table. The children feel, smell and name them. Everyone thinks about where different vegetables grow (above or below ground), then prepare a box, which is placed upside down on the floor with the open end to the floor. The box represents a vegetable patch. A hole is cut into one side to put in those vegetables that grow underground.

One child closes his eyes and is given a vegetable to hold. He now has to guess what that vegetable is. For example, he might say, 'It's a carrot. Carrots grow underground'. He then puts the carrot into the box. Or he could say, 'That's a pea. Peas grow above ground'. He then puts the pea on top of the box. Then the next child takes his turn.

When all the vegetables have been sorted, the children line up behind each other in front of a mat or soft blanket. The first child says, 'I like eating … What about you?' After he has said what he likes, he does a somersault. All the children get a turn.

Then you could get the children to say, 'I don't like … What about you?' or you could ask the children, one by one, 'Do you like eating …?' You could then play a memory game with the children. 'The vegetables that grow underground are not visible. Who can remember them?'

Once the children have mastered the different vegetable names, the vegetables are washed and cut into bite-sized pieces. Each child now has to taste what he has in his mouth with his eyes closed. The children could also experiment with holding their noses while tasting a vegetable, to help them work out that tasting is more difficult without a sense of smell. Or maybe they could try to guess different vegetables by smell only, tasting them with their eyes closed.

Any leftover vegetables can be used to make vegetable soup. Even this could be built into a little fairy story: Grandmother visits a Prince (or any suitable puppet), and tells him that she would love to cook a vegetable soup, but unfortunately she has forgotten which vegetables can be used to make a soup. The children help her, and tell her the names of the different vegetables. The Prince enjoys the soup and then takes the children on an adventurous journey.

Variation
Fruit could be substituted for vegetables and a 'Fruit Harvest' game played.

Everyone thinks about what sorts of plants carry these fruits and where they grow. (Remember that the question, 'Above or below ground?' is redundant here.) Instead of vegetable soup, you could prepare a fruit salad.

Aims: developing tactile perception, vocabulary, use of the prepositions *above* and *below*, developing a sense of smell, a sense of taste, body coordination, proprioception, memory, and encouraging children to enjoy talking

Materials: different kinds of vegetables (or fruit), box, mat or soft blanket. In addition: knife, plate or bowl, saucepan, cooker, spoon, hand puppets (Grandmother and Prince, etc)

(**6**) Fruit thieves

The children pretend to be thieves. They build a den in which to hide and take it in turns to steal apples from a box behind a fence. Put up a piece of string to mark the fence and place a table behind the fence with the box of apples (or suitable substitute) on it. The table should be quite a distance behind the fence so that each child has to stretch well forward in order to reach an apple. The thief has to creep up to the fence, steal an apple, and quickly run back to his den and whisper to his boss how many he has stolen. For example, 'I could only steal one apple!'

One child pretends to be the farmer, who is keeping a close eye on the fence. If the thief touches the fence, the farmer will chase and try to catch the robber. If the farmer manages to catch the thief before he can disappear into his den, the thief turns into the farmer and the farmer into the thief.

Aims: developing body awareness, tactile awareness and perception, sense of balance, agility, speed

Materials: string, box of apples (or substitute), table, blanket

Variation

The thieves' favourite orchard has been fenced off (use some string or thin rope). There is only just enough room for someone to crawl between the ground and the fence. Now, one thief after the other tries to steal some fruit. Each time, the thief says first what he is going to steal: 'I am going to fetch a juicy pear!', and so on. At the end, if the fruit is real, the thieves are allowed to eat their stolen goods.

If the string is touched, an alarm bell starts ringing, *trrr*, and the fruit has to be left behind. (That thief can have another go later.) The other children are responsible for making the alarm sound, so they have to watch the thief and the string closely.

Aims: developing body awareness, agility, suppleness, learning the names of different kinds of fruit, practising the consonant cluster *tr*

Variation materials: string or thin rope, fruit

7   Fruit memory

For this game, you need some picture cards showing fruit. Each kind of fruit has its own set of cards. In each set, each card depicts a certain quantity of the fruit on it, depending on a child's understanding of quantity. For example, the apple set will contain a card with one apple, a card with two apples, and so on.

The children take it in turns to be transformed into a magician by the adult, who rubs a magic wand over each child's face and hands, while saying, 'Hocus-pocus, fiddle-dee-dee, a magician you will be!' The remaining children help say the magic spell.

Then the child is given the magic wand and uses it to turn one fruit into many. This is how he does it. All of the cards showing only one piece of fruit are put in a pile, while the cards with more than one piece of fruit are spread out around the room between lots of balls or other obstacles. The child magician takes a card from the pile (for example, an apple) and, while he is walking around the room looking for a matching card without knocking into any of the obstacles, he says a magic spell, such as, 'Hocus-pocus, ten a penny – abracadabra! One becomes many!' When he has found the card corresponding to the one in his hand, he picks it up and puts it with its partner card, saying 'I have made three [or four, two, etc] apples appear!'

Aims: developing tactile perception, room orientation, agility, practising singular and plural, developing memory, visual perception, articulation

Materials: picture cards with drawings or representations of different fruit (one singular and one plural card for each fruit), balls or other obstacles, magic wand

) **Still life exercise with grapes**

The children sit in a circle on the floor. In response to an acoustic signal, they all close their eyes and are only allowed to open them when they hear the signal for the second time. While the children have their eyes shut, a plate of grapes is placed in the middle of the circle.

Then the signal sounds again and the children look at the plate. One at a time, the children are invited to say what they are thinking, the ideas that occur to them, and any related memories they may have. Then the bunch of grapes is picked up by its stalk and put into the hands of one of the children. Each child should get an opportunity to hold the bunch of grapes and pass it on, holding the stalk. What does a bunch of grapes feel like?

At the end, each child picks a grape and lets the grape talk about itself: 'I am round; I am sweet; I am sour; I am juicy; I would make excellent grape juice; you could make wine with me; I grew on a sunny hill slope; I was looked after well by the winegrower', and so on. Then the grapes are washed and tried by everyone.

(From an idea by Maria Montessori.)

Aims: developing acoustic perception, calming down, sensitising power of perception, developing the ability to be gentle, awakening feelings of care and respect, developing tactile awareness, feeling mass and weight, developing imagination

Materials: plate, bunch of grapes, a means to create an acoustic signal

9 Full or empty?

For this game, you need several empty cardboard boxes or shoeboxes. Some of the boxes are filled with toy bricks or similar objects. The children know that they are going to try and remember which ones are full. The boxes are shuffled while everyone watches. The group pretends it is running a fruit stall at the market and has only a couple of boxes of fruit left, because so much has already been sold.

Now it is time to guess which box is which. The first child points to one of the boxes and says, 'This box is still full'. Check whether they are correct: lift the box and check its weight, then look inside. Are they correct? Later you could also add a few half-full boxes. Let the children see for themselves whether they are correct.

Aims: developing visual perception, perception of weight, working on the concepts of *full, empty, half-full*

Materials: cardboard boxes or shoe boxes, building blocks or other objects to put in the boxes

10 Hedgehog walk

Make a hedgehog from cardboard, together with a turning disc with a serrated edge to represent its legs. This is how to do it:

◆ Cut the hedgehog and a small cog-wheel out of cardboard.
◆ Using scissors, a hole is punched in the hedgehog and the cog-wheel.
◆ The cog-wheel is then placed behind the hedgehog so the two holes match up. Fasten the holes together using a paper fastener pushed through from the front and bent apart at the back of the hedgehog.
◆ The hedgehog is now able to 'walk'. If it walks along the floor through a carpet of previously collected dried leaves, it will make a lovely rustling noise.

(Creative idea from: Düsseldorfer E, 1996, *Das neue Bastelbuch für Kinder*, Bassermann, Niedernhausen, p174.)

Start playing. One child closes his eyes, while another lets the hedgehog go for a walk. With his eyes closed, the first child is supposed to sense where the hedgehog is walking: 'The hedgehog is walking over my tummy [my head, my leg, my hand, my index finger]'.

At the end of the game, prepare some leaves for the hedgehog to go into hibernation. You could put paint on

previously collected autumn leaves and make leaf prints using white sheets of paper then cut out the individual leaves when they are dry. The hedgehog can go to sleep under the heap of leaves. In spring, the hedgehog becomes active again.

Aims: developing tactile awareness and perception, finger skills, body awareness, consolidating body part names, developing fine motor skills, hand-eye coordination

Materials: cardboard, paper fasteners, autumn leaves, paints, paper, safety scissors

11 The hedgehog is hibernating

One child pretends to be the hedgehog, lying on the floor and closing his eyes. The other children are given leaves (you could use paper napkins as substitutes) and, one at a time, they carefully place a 'leaf' on top of the hedgehog and wish him a good sleep. The hedgehog could also make specific requests as to where he would like the leaves to be placed.

After a while, the hedgehog remembers that he has to do something before he finally goes into hibernation. He tells the other children what he has to do (for example, visit a friend to say goodbye, help the squirrels to collect some nuts, show the cat where he has put the milk plate, and so on) and gets up quickly. Then it is the next child's turn to pretend to be the hedgehog.

Aims: stimulating awareness of touch, naming body parts, improving body awareness, developing imagination, enjoying talking

Materials: paper napkins or leaves

12) **Autumn 'feely' road**

The group goes on a walk in the woods in autumn to collect things: horse chestnuts, acorns, leaves, fir cones, beechnuts, nuts, roots, stones, etc. Then they sort the items into different shallow boxes or box lids and line up the boxes, one behind the other. A child walks barefoot with eyes closed alongside the boxes, and tries to feel the content of the boxes using one foot only. The other foot stays outside the box to help the child balance – in this way, fragile things don't get broken and the children don't hurt themselves on the harder or pricklier objects. What do the different things feel like?

The order of the boxes is changed regularly. Which child can recall the content of the different boxes when they get to the end of the road? They can also use their hands to guess.

Variation
To vary the game, you could also use non-breakable everyday household items such as sponges, spoons, tea towels, marbles, pens, cotton wool, buttons, clothes pegs, and so on, to fill the box lids.

Aims: developing tactile awareness and perception, body awareness, vocabulary, body control, balance, memory

Materials: different materials from the woods (or household objects), shallow boxes or box lids

13) Can you feel the conker?

One child stretches out on his back on a blanket (arms up), and closes his eyes. Another child puts a horse chestnut under the blanket, and gives the instruction, 'Start rolling! Where can you feel the conker?' Stretched out, the first child now rolls across the blanket. He tries to feel the conker and tells the others where he can feel it. The other children observe carefully, so that they notice which body part touches the conker under the blanket.

Aims: developing tactile awareness, body control, articulation, body awareness, naming body parts

Materials: blanket, horse chestnut

14 It is snowing

The children get together in pairs. The adult tells a story and the children act out the story, using their partner's back as a stage and making accompanying noises:

◆ Looking out of the window, you can see individual, thick, heavy snowflakes (gently tap individual fingers on your partner's back).

◆ The snow gets heavier and denser (tap faster and faster).

◆ Now there is a proper snowstorm (rub the palms of your flat hands across your partner's back, and accompany this with *shshsh* sounds).

◆ There is lots of snow everywhere. 'Enough snow to go sledging', Crispin is thinking. He gets his sledge and walks up the hill (two fingers of one hand 'walk' up your partner's back, accompanied by tongue-clicking sounds, while two fingers of the other hand drag up the sledge behind).

◆ Crispin has made it to the top and is looking forward to sledging down. 'One, two, three, go!', and off he goes (two palms stroke quickly downwards, accompanied by *shshsh*).

◆ Crispin marches back up. After several repetitions he gets tired and stomps off home (two fingers of one hand walk back down your partner's back, accompanied by tongue-clicking, while two fingers of the other hand drag the sledge back down again).

◆ Then swap roles. Maybe a child can retell the story or tell a similar story.

Aims: developing tactile awareness, auditory attention, contact with others, finger motor activity, coordination, articulation of *sh*, oro-motor skills

---

Materials: none

(**15**) Footsteps

The children get together in pairs. One child chooses a colour and paints his feet with finger-paint, describes what this feels like, and then stands on a piece of paper. Afterwards, the child washes his feet and dries them carefully. The child's partner helps with the painting and washing. Then it is the second child's turn, and the first child helps.

Afterwards, cut out everyone's footprints – each child will have a left and a right print – and draw a face on the footprints. Once they have dried, all the footprints are mixed up, and everybody, in turn, looks for their own two footprints. Then the footprints have a conversation with each other.

At the end of the game, line up the footprints on the floor to make a road. As each child walks the road, he is the only one allowed to step on the footprints.

Aims: developing tactile awareness and perception, social interaction, visual perception, enjoying talking, developing imagination, body control, sense of balance

Materials: finger-paints, paper, washing-up bowl, towel, pens

16 Cold – colder – coldest

In winter, it is very cold. Everyone has to try and find out how good their hands are at assessing temperature. Three containers are filled with water, using a ladle. The first is filled with cold water. The second is filled with even colder water and the third with iced water (water with ice cubes). Now one child closes his eyes while the containers are swapped around. The child then has to feel the water with his hands, and assign the adjectives *cold, colder, coldest* to the three containers. Later, try the same game, but use warm or comfortably hot water instead.

Aims: using the adjectives *cold, warm* and *hot*, and their comparative and superlative forms, developing tactile awareness, hand-eye coordination (ladling water)

Materials: three identical containers (mugs, glasses or similar), cold/warm/hot water

17 Father Christmas

Using a picture of Father Christmas, talk about what he looks like and what he carries around with him, then tell the story of St Nicholas. Get the children to make some of the things which are important to his story before you play this game.

Everyone takes turns to be Father Christmas. The others could learn a Father Christmas poem and recite it to him, or they could sing him a Christmas song. Father Christmas tells his own story and discusses with the children what good deeds they could do, people they could help, things that good children should not do and what might be particularly nice for specific children to do.

Then one child after another closes their eyes and waits for Father Christmas to put some raisins in their hands. Every child first has to guess how many raisins he has in his hands. At the end, each child is given enough raisins to bring the number they are holding up to five or ten (depending on what number you want to focus on) when you ask the question, 'How many more raisins do you still need?' (The children should be told *before* the game that everybody will receive the same amount!)

Aims: developing auditory attention, visual perception, skilfulness (making things), memory, phonological awareness (rhymes), enjoying talking, reflecting on the behaviour of individual children, developing tactile awareness, understanding of quantity concepts

Variation
Place one, two or three raisins on each child's tongue. The child has to guess the correct number on his tongue simply by feel. Children can then check for themselves by looking in the mirror. Regardless of whether they have guessed the correct number or not they will definitely enjoy eating the raisins.

Aims: developing tactile awareness, awareness of the inside of the mouth, understanding of quantity

Materials: raisins (or substitute), possibly arts and crafts materials to make the things to accompany the Father Christmas story, and a Father Christmas picture

18 The four seasons

PART 1

First, recite with the children the following poem:

> Springtime makes the flowers grow
> Summer brings the clover
> Grapes in autumn
> Winter, snow –
> Then the year is over.

Now the children act out the words. Divide them into four groups of equal number, each group representing one season and each standing in a different corner of the room.

- Spring: together, the children mime a flower by making their arms into a petal shape.
- Summer: four children represent a lucky clover leaf, while another pretends to be the stalk.
- Autumn: together, the children form a bunch of grapes.
- Winter: the children pretend to be skiers, miming a skiing movement.

Then everyone recites the poem together, with every group performing the actions for their season. Every time the poem is repeated, the groups should change places. Repeat the poem at least four times, so that every

group gets an opportunity to represent each season at least once.

Aims: consolidating understanding of quantity, developing tactile awareness, body awareness, left/right awareness ('skiing'), auditory attention, reaction, memory, room orientation

> **Materials for Part 1:** none

PART 2

Each child is given four small pieces of paper or index cards, and is asked to draw four pictures representing the four seasons (flowers, clover, grapes, snow). Then the children turn these into four signs by sticking a plastic straw or a small stick on the back of the pictures. Now the poem about the four seasons is recited (see above), and the children have to hold up the corresponding signs for the different seasons.

Afterwards, the signs are allocated to the four corners of the room. The children stand in the middle of the room and have to react to the name of the season that is called out by running to the matching corner. Once all children have arrived in the corner, they get together in pairs and clap out the rhythm of the name of the season by clapping their palms together: for instance, 'This is win-ter', will be 4 claps.

Aims: naming the four seasons and assigning pictures to them, developing auditory attention and reaction, room orientation, tactile awareness, speech rhythm.

Materials for Part 2: small pieces of paper or index cards, straws or small wooden sticks, coloured pens, glue or sticky tape

19   Let's turn ourselves into magic animals

The children crawl through a magic tunnel. To make the tunnel, chairs could be lined up one behind the other. Alternatively, the children could build the tunnel themselves by standing with their legs apart, one behind the other. The last child in the row crawls through the tunnel (if possible without touching the sides) to the back and then stands as part of the tunnel at the front again.

Once all the children have crawled through the tunnel they are turned into animals by a magic spell. The spell could be 'Shrimmel, shrammel, shree – bees you will be!' accompanied by the beat of a drum. The spell always lasts until the next drum beat. The first part of the spell is said together by everybody. The children then have to make movements suited to the animals:

◆ The bee should hum and try to sting.
◆ The snakes slither in the direction of the snake charmer.
◆ The horses jump over obstacles. (See materials box for suggestions.)
◆ The tigers prowl through the jungle.
◆ Bear cubs roll around on their sides.
◆ Monkeys climb or swing off a rope.
◆ Cats slurp milk (the tongue is moved in and out in a relaxed way), or hiss and chase mice (trying to catch rolling balls).

◆ Lions pounce!
◆ Frogs jump about trying to catch flies.
◆ Storks strut about and chase frogs: to do this, the storks are only allowed to jump about on one leg and the frogs have to 'frog-hop'. Go with the children's ideas!

Aims: developing tactile awareness, switching from one movement to another, developing imagination, gross and fine motor skills, body awareness, oro-motor skills, appropriate articulation of different speech sounds (voiced *z* and voiceless *s*, *ch*, *quack*), appropriate articulation of consonant clusters when saying the spell, acoustic perception, ability to react

Materials: Hoops, beanbags, mats, rope, big ball, drum

(20) Where is the beetle resting?

Fingers represent the beetle. One child lies on the floor and closes his eyes. Another child alternately runs their index finger and then their middle finger (the 'beetle') over the body of the child on the floor while making a clicking noise – *k-k-k*! and says, 'I'm a creepy-crawly chap, but now I'm going to have a nap!' – and then stops the finger somewhere on the other child's body. The child on the floor now has to identify and describe where the beetle is sitting.

Aims: developing articulation, especially the sound /k/ and the consonant cluster *cr*, tactile perception and awareness, physical interaction, body awareness, finger skills, naming body parts

Materials: none

(**21**) Waking up the spring flowers

All the children pretend to be flowers and prepare for spring. To begin with, all flowers are still in the ground, so the children need to lie curled up on the floor with their eyes closed. Spring (an adult or a chosen child) wakes the flowers from their winter sleep by lightly touching them. Any child that has been woken slowly makes himself taller and taller, until he stands up like a beautiful flower. The arms form the petals. Everyone watches the different beautiful flowers and the children describe in more detail what kind of flower they are (colour, shape, size, scent, and so on).

For the following game, there are three signals (visual or acoustic) – one for sun, one for rain and one for night-time.

If the signal for *rain* is given, the children have to close up their petals by putting their hands together straight above their heads, and then recite a rain rhyme, such as 'Pitter, patter raindrops', or 'It's raining, it's pouring, the old man is snoring'. If, in addition, there is a storm, the flowers could sway backwards and forwards while standing.

If the signal for *sun* is given, the children open up their petals and say, 'Sunshine, sunshine, wake up all the little flowers!' As the sun moves in the sky, the flowers could

turn to the sun. To do this, the children shou'
their upper bodies, not their feet, which re
roots.

If the signal for *night* is given, the children close up their
petals and sit down on the floor with their legs crossed
(without using their hands), let their heads flop down
towards the floor, and say, 'We gently close our eyes and
quietly say good night'.

Aims: developing tactile awareness, imagination, body
control, body coordination, articulation, memory, ability
to react, auditory and visual attention

Materials: possibly material for visual or acoustic
signals

22) Cat, bird, mouse and dog

The children get together in pairs. One child from each pair sits down on the floor and closes his eyes. There are different visual signals for each animal (cat, bird, mouse and dog).

◆ If the signal for *cat* is given, the partner who is standing rubs his head on the sitting child, pretending to be a cat.

◆ If the signal for *bird* is given, the partner has to place some fingers on the head of the sitting child, who now has to guess how many birds (or fingers) are sitting on his head.

◆ If the signal for *mouse* is given, the partner has to run his index and middle finger along the sitting child's arm.

◆ If the signal for *dog* is given, the partner leans on the shoulders of the sitting child, using his hands.

Each time the sitting child is touched by the other child's fingers, he tells everyone else which animal his partner is pretending to be, and whether the touch was enjoyable or not. At the end, the children make up a story involving a cat, a bird, a mouse and a dog, then act out the story as role-play.

Aims: stimulating tactile awareness, tolerating and identifying touch, facilitating physical interaction, developing the ability to react, memory, visual attention, finger skills, imagination

Materials: possibly material for visual signals

23) Molly the cat

The adult tells a story about the cat, Molly. The children listen and dramatise the story through movement.

◆ Molly lies curled up in the garden. Then the sun starts shining directly onto Molly's little nose (the adult touches every 'cat' on the nose, using a feather).

◆ Molly twitches her whiskers and has to sneeze. Now she has woken herself up. She stretches her front paws as far forward as possible and her back paws as far back as possible and arches her back.

◆ Slowly, she walks to her feeding bowl and slurps some milk (a broad and relaxed tongue is moved back and forth between the lips).

◆ Then she cleans herself and licks her tongue across her mouth. She also tries to lick her nose and her chin.

She thinks to herself, 'A mouse would be nice now!' She creeps up to the mousehole and waits for the mouse to come out. All of a sudden, the storyteller rolls a number of marbles (to represent the mice), corresponding to the number of children in the room. Watch out mice! Molly catches a mouse.

Aims: developing tactile awareness, auditory attention, ability to react, oro-motor skills, speed, following verbal instructions

Materials: marbles

24 Rainy weather!

Every child finds a partner. The adult reports on the weather, and every child acts out the weather which is described on his partner's back. This is what the weather is like:

◆ The sun is shining. (Both hands are placed flat on the partner's back.)

◆ A cloud is moving in front of the sun. (Use both hands to rub along the back.)

◆ It starts to rain (Tap the fingertips across the back and reinforce by articulating *t, t, t.*)

◆ It starts to get a little bit windy. (Stroke the hands across the back and make a gentle *sss* sound.)

◆ Then the wind becomes stronger. (Stroke the hands across the back with firm and fast movements, while making a *shshsh* sound.)

◆ The rain becomes stronger. (Tap across the back in short bursts and articulate *t, t, t.*)

◆ Now there is also thunder. (Drum the fists on the back – not too hard! – and make a *p-ch* sound.)

◆ Water is tipping down from the sky now. (Use both fists to stroke quickly down next to the spine while articulating *shshsh.*)

◆ Now the sun starts to come through again and warms everyone up. (Flat hands are placed on the back.)

◆ The wind chases away the rainy weather (rub both flat hands across the back) and the storm is over …

◆ The alarm clock sounds *trrr* – it was only a dream. Swap roles.

Aims: developing tactile awareness and perception, body awareness, social interaction, articulation (particularly the sounds *t*, *sh*, *s* and *tr*), acoustic perception, ability to react

Materials: none

25 Riding a bike

It is a warm spring day, and we are going on a bike ride! In pairs, the children lie on the floor with the soles of their feet touching and move their legs as if they were riding a bike. Their eyes are kept closed while doing this. The adult tells a story about a bike ride, for example: 'We are riding across a bumpy road – now we are pedalling up the hill – we have to use lots of strength to pedal – we've made it! – now we are just cycling along …). Once in a while, make a noise to indicate a bursting tyre by clapping, making a *pfff* sound, or clicking the tongue. If the children hear this noise, they have to stop immediately, stand up and pump up the tyre. One child in each pair pretends to be the tyre by crouching down on the floor, while the other child makes a pumping movement and the pumping sound (*f-f-f* or *sh-sh-sh*). The child who is pretending to be the tyre gets bigger with every pumping sound until he is on all fours. The adult checks whether the pumps are working (has the correct *f* or *sh* been articulated?). Then the roles are reversed after the next burst tyre.

Aims: developing body awareness, tactile awareness, body coordination, auditory attention, articulation of the sounds *f* and *sh*

Materials: none

(26) Chicks and vultures

One child pretends to be the vulture and a second child is the chick. The remaining children hold hands and pretend to be hens who, together, try to protect the chick. The chick is scared and calls *cheep cheep cheep*, and the vulture angrily calls *crar crar crar*. If the vulture touches the chick, the chick becomes the vulture.

Aims: articulating *cr* and *ch*, facilitating the ability to react, agility, tactile awareness, speed

Materials: none

27 Bird feathers

The birds have lost lots of feathers while building their nests. A feather is hidden somewhere in the room for each child – they have to find this and then keep it in the air for as long as possible by blowing it. First the children take turns to tell the others where they would like to blow their feathers – for example, 'I am going to blow my feather onto the table!' – after which, through measured blowing, they try to get their feathers to the intended destinations. They could also try to blow while making a *sh* sound, representing the wind.

Then the children get together in pairs. One child closes his eyes and the other child touches him with the feather. He now has to describe the place where he has been touched.

Next, all the children crouch down on the floor in one corner of the room and try to blow the feather to the other side of the room while crawling. This could also be turned into a race.

Finally, each child creates own his paradise bird. To do this, children are given paper, pens and glue. The real feather is stuck somewhere on the bird and could become a magic feather. What sort of magic power does the feather give its bird?

Aims: developing visual perception, oro-motor skills, possibly the sound *sh*, developing tactile perception, naming body parts, developing social interaction, facilitating proprioception, imagination

Materials: feathers, paper, pens, coloured pencils or crayons, glue

28 How many eggs are in the nest?

One child puts five fingers of one hand on the head of another child and asks the first question:

Question: 'Is the crow perching?' – Answer: 'Yes!'
Question: 'Has it got a nest?' – Answer: 'Yes!'
Question: 'How many eggs has it got?' – Answer: [number of eggs]

While asking this last question, the child can either leave all five fingers on the other child's head or lift some of them away. The other child has to guess or sense how many fingers are touching his head. Once he has guessed the correct number, he is asked: 'Hard or soft eggs?' Depending on the child's answer and the number of eggs, he is given hard (but not too hard!) or soft pats on the head.

Aims: tolerating physical contact, developing tactile perception, articulation, understanding of quantity, body awareness

Materials: none

29 Oh, a puddle!

You could start this activity with a story about a child who does not look where he is going. Then put some gym mats on top of each other and pretend they are a puddle.

One child starts the game by walking towards the mats with his eyes closed, or his head facing upwards, until he gets to the mats and lets himself fall on top of them. Then he gets up again and tells the others: 'A moment ago, my trousers were still clean – now they're all dirty'.

The children could also talk about things that they are pretending to have on them after falling in the puddle, for example: 'Just now, this envelope was clean, now it is really dirty!'

Each child should get as many turns as possible. The children could also guess how many steps they will need to take to get to the puddle.

Aims: practising the adjectives clean/dirty, facilitating room orientation, body awareness, imagination

Materials: gym mats

(30) Snake or stake?

The group puts a blanket on the floor and gets together in pairs. One child closes his eyes. His partner puts either a rope or a thin building block under the blanket. The other child then rolls length-wise across the blanket with his arms stretched out over his head. Afterwards, the child has to describe what he felt under the blanket, in response to the question, 'Snake or stake?', and can then check to see whether or not he was correct.

If the child felt the block, he has to build a tower ('the stake') from four or five toy bricks with his eyes closed. If he felt the rope, he has to close his eyes and make a snake by attaching four or five clothes pegs to each other. His partner gives him the relevant materials for the task. In this way, one child has to try to articulate correctly, and the other child has to discriminate correctly between the two words. Then the roles are swapped over.

Aims: developing proprioception, auditory discrimination of similar sounding words, tactile awareness, gentleness, finger skills, room orientation

---

Materials: blanket, thin building block, rope, five building blocks, five clothes pegs

---

(**31**) My fingers can feel

A selection of different objects, whose names involve a
target sound that needs to be practised, is put in a 'feely'
bag. The children have to feel the objects, name them,
take them out of the bag, check whether their fingers
have felt correctly, and then say: 'There was a … in the
bag'. Encourage the group to talk about the different
attributes of the objects: 'What does the object feel like?
How did you recognise it so quickly?'

Aims: developing tactile perception, articulation,
practising vocabulary relating to the attributes of the
objects used

Materials: different objects, 'feely' bag

(32) 'Feely' wall

Attach a large piece of cardboard or a pin board to the wall, so it is within reach of the children, and then stick different objects to the board for the children to feel. The objects should have different characteristics (big, small, rough, smooth, hard, spiky, pointed, etc).

Then a blindfold child is led to the wall by another child – either by their hand, or by being given instructions, such as *left, right, straight on, one step,* etc. Using only his hands, the blindfold child has to find a previously specified object from amongst the selection of objects on the board, or he could be led to a particular item and, again using only his hands, has to guess what it is. The 'feely' wall can be extended by adding new things once in a while.

Aims: developing tactile perception, room orientation, vocabulary

---

Materials: cardboard or pin board, different objects to be felt

---

33) Can your feet feel?

The children are barefoot. A selection of objects has been prepared to be looked at, felt and named. One child closes his eyes, and another child places one of the objects in front of his feet and asks: 'Let your feet feel, do, then tell me what lies in front of you?' The child asking the question claps his hands in rhythm with his speech.

Aims: developing tactile awareness and perception, articulation, rhythm awareness, vocabulary development

Materials: different objects to be felt

(34) Small acrobatics

Each child is given a carpet tile or a newspaper. In response to a given instruction, the children have to touch the tile or newspaper with the body part named. The instructions could be: use only your heels, only three fingers, only tip-toes, only your left shoulder, right index finger and left foot, only your forehead, only your chin, right elbow and right knee, and so on. Go with the children's ideas!

Afterwards, all of the carpet tiles are arranged in a circle, and the children walk around the circle reciting a rhyme, while moving from tile to tile, following the rhythm of the rhyme (for example, one tile per syllable). The speed of reciting the rhyme is gradually increased, which means that the children have to walk faster and faster, until everybody ends up in a muddle.

Aims: developing body awareness, naming body parts, developing gross motor skills, coordination, tactile awareness, improving rhythmical perception, memory training

---

Materials: carpet tiles (which provide a nice tactile sensation) or newspaper pages

---

35   Birthday present in the sandpit

Whenever one of the children has a birthday, little presents are wrapped in silver foil or film containers and buried in the sand. The children use their hands to dig out the presents.

Instead of sand you could also use a bowl of corn, perhaps hiding wooden beads amongst the corn and getting the children to find them. Each bead can be exchanged for a small present.

Aims: developing tactile awareness and perception

Materials: sandpit or bowl with corn, film containers or silver foil, wooden beads, small presents

36 Puzzle pieces in the sand

Individual puzzle pieces are hidden in film containers, and the containers are buried in sand. Each child is allowed to find one container. Then the children assemble the puzzle together. The pieces could contain a message, such as a route description, a treasure map, or a map for finding the next meeting point. In this way, lots of opportunities for talking are created, and the game can continue indefinitely.

Aims: stimulating tactile awareness, developing tactile perception, visual perception, imagination, enjoying talking

Materials: sandpit, film containers, puzzle pieces

37) Sand pictures

Using glue, simple shapes (circle, cross, triangle, square, line, star, sun, snake, house, etc) are drawn onto small pieces of cardboard. With young children, the adult could first outline the shape with a pencil for the children to follow in glue. Then the cardboard piece is pressed onto the sand. The sand will only stick to the glue, and you will end up with shapes that can be felt. The children have to recognise and name the shapes through touch while blindfolded.

Variation

This game is similar to 'Chinese Whispers'. The children sit in a line, one behind the other. One child can draw the shape he has felt (from the sandpit) on the back of another child using his finger. That child has to guess which shape has been drawn on his back. The next child in turn, draws the shape he has felt on the back of the child in front of *him*. What will the shape be like by the time it is drawn on the first child's back?

The game can continue indefinitely. Whoever is sitting at the front of the line can pick out a shape from the sand and sit down at the back and begin the whole game again. Younger children, who are not yet able to name the different shapes, could be shown a selection for them to select the one they think they have felt.

Aims: developing hand-eye coordination, tactile awareness and perception, social interaction, naming different basic shapes

---

Materials: pieces of cardboard, glue, fine sand

(38)   Funny reflexes

This game is played in pairs. One partner demonstrates the reflexes, while the other triggers them by touching different body parts:

- ◆ Touch the back of the head: the tongue shoots out.
- ◆ Pull the right ear lobe: the tongue shoots to the right.
- ◆ Pull the left ear lobe: the tongue shoots to the left.
- ◆ Press the nose: the tongue goes up in the direction of the nose.
- ◆ Pull both ear lobes simultaneously: the child makes a smiley face.
- ◆ Pull the nose to one side; the tongue moves quickly between the left and right corners of the mouth, accompanied by a noise (which you could call the 'tongue alarm clock')
- ◆ Touch the highest point on the head: the tongue is placed behind the upper front teeth (you could say that the 'tongue goes up to the first floor').
- ◆ Touch between neck and chin: the tongue is placed behind the lower front teeth (you could say that the 'tongue goes down to the cellar').
- ◆ Clap both hands together: the mouth closes.

(Idea from: Stöcklin-Meier S, 1995, *Eins, zwei, drei – ritsche, ratsche, rei. Kinderspielverse zum Necken, Lachen, Hüpfen, Tanzen*, Ravensburger Buchverlag, Ravensburg.)

Aims: improving oro-motor skills and tongue movement, facilitating the ability to react quickly, developing memory, tactile awareness and perception

Materials: none

Games for developing proprioception

Precise articulation in order to produce speech sounds involves specific movements of the mouth, tongue and lips. Therefore good articulation requires good proprioception. However, inaccurate information and feedback with regard to muscle tension and change in position of the joints leads to poor self-awareness and poor proprioception. In turn, this impacts on fine motor, as well as oro-motor, skills.

The following games are predominantly designed to stimulate the children's sense of proprioception, and thus contribute to the facilitation of speech and language development.

39 And who are you?

This game is about singing whilst moving a ball around simultaneously. It would be best if the movements with the ball matched the rhythm of the song.

All the children form a big circle. The game leader starts by taking a ball and singing,

‘My name is [Maria]’.

This is accompanied by some sort of movement with the ball (suggestions below). The adult then rolls the ball to a child across from her and sings,

‘And what is your name?’

Then that child, in turn, has to sing his name, make the appropriate movement and pass the ball to yet another child.

Suggested movements to accompany the singing:

◆ Press the ball to the chest on ‘my’
◆ Press the ball to the head on ‘name’
◆ Hold the ball out in front with both hands on ‘is’
◆ Sit on the ball on ‘[Maria]’
◆ Roll the ball to another child on ‘and who are you?’

When everyone has had a turn, the wording used in the game is reversed. Again the adult starts, making specific movements with the ball (see suggestions below). He then rolls the ball to a child, singing:

'You are [Julia] and who do you know?'

Suggested movements for the second part of the game:

◆ Hold the ball with both hands and stretch the arms in the direction of the child on 'you'
◆ Press the ball on the head on 'are'
◆ Sit on the ball on 'Julia'
◆ Roll the ball to another child on 'and who do you know?'

Aims: developing touch awareness, proprioception, hand-eye coordination, memory, learning other children's names

Materials: ball

40 Tummy, back or side?

The children form a circle and close their eyes. One child goes to the middle of the circle and hides under a blanket. Then he calls out: 'Which side am I lying on – on my tummy, back or side?' Then the other children try to work out by looking and touching whether the child is lying on their tummy, back or side.

If there are enough blankets, this game can also be played in pairs. Children check whether they have guessed correctly by pulling off the blanket.

Variation
The child who is trying to guess the position of the child under the blanket, has to copy the position himself. When he has finished, the blanket is taken away and the children check whether or not both are lying in the same way. This game naturally creates lots of opportunities for talking.

Aims: developing body awareness, tactile perception, visual perception, touch sensation, gentleness, naming body parts

Materials: one blanket, or a blanket for each pair of children

41 That's me!

Each child lies down on a large sheet of brown paper and the adult draws an outline of the child's body onto the paper. If the children are old enough, they can get together in pairs and draw each other's outline. Then each child completes their outline by adding missing features such as hair, face, tummy button, knee folds, finger nails, toe nails, as well as unique features such as birthmarks or scars.

Once the outlines are complete, one child from each pair lies down next to their outline. Their partner gently presses a cork somewhere on the body of the child who is lying down. That child then has to remember where they have been touched, take the cork and place it exactly on the same place on their paper outline. Then the roles are swapped.

Aims: tactile-kinaesthetic stimulation, developing body awareness, accurate body observation, naming body parts, vocabulary development, developing kinaesthetic memory, tolerating physical contact, developing hand-eye control while independently tracing body outlines

Materials: brown paper, pens, corks

42 Holiday experiences

First of all, everybody talks about what they did in the holidays. Then the children pretend to take the train back on holiday again. Everybody is given a ribbon or scarf which represents the wheels of the train. The children snake around the room in a line, moving the ribbon/scarf in circles. A rope could also be used for the children to hold on to with their other hand, so that all the carriages are linked together. During the ride, everyone can imitate the noise of the carriage, saying *sh-sh-sh*.

The children can take it in turns to stop the train by shouting '*Stop!*' Whoever stops the train mimes something they experienced during their holiday (for example, eating, drinking, licking ice-cream, swimming, diving, climbing, cycling, going on a boat, painting, building sandcastles, playing ball, playing badminton, etc). The other children try to guess what the child is miming. Or the child can choose to tell a story whilst doing the actions. At the end of the game, everyone rides back into the present.

On the way home, the adult pretends to be the train driver and checks whether each carriage is working correctly (in other words, if every child can articulate *sh* appropriately). If the carriage is not working properly (a child may need to practise articulating the *sh* sound), it has to go into the garage to be fixed

Aims: developing body coordination, auditory perception, imagination, articulation of the *sh* sound, ability to react to a signal, ability to observe and watch, self-confidence

Materials: ribbons or scarves

43 Picking apples and pears

The children use chalk to draw hopscotch squares on the ground. At the end of the 'path' lies a castle. In the castle, there are a normal dice and a dice with apples and pears. According to the rules agreed, the child has to hop to the castle using straddle vaults or standing jumps. When he has arrived at the castle, he is allowed to throw both the dice. The dice tell the child what he is allowed to pick (apples or pears), and how many. Then the child announces: 'I am allowed to pick two pears', and climbs up the tree (which could be a rope ladder, a wall ladder, a stepladder, or even a real tree) to pick his fruit. Pretend apples and pears (eg, plastic fruit) are contained in a little bag which has been attached to the tree. However, the child is not allowed to look inside the bag – he is only allowed to feel. If he takes the wrong fruit, it has to go back in the bag. For older children, you could also use shapes cut out of cardboard. The game continues until every child has got a previously determined number of apples and pears.

Aims: developing coordination, body control, understanding of quantity concepts, tactile perception, formulating sentences, articulation of *p* (*pears, pick*)

Materials: chalk, number dice, dice with apples and pears, rope ladder (or wall ladder, stepladder, or real tree), pretend apples and pears or cardboard shapes, small bag

44 How much fruit would you like?

Draw a hopscotch outline and let the children jump according to agreed rules (standing jump, straddle jump, one-leg jump, two-leg jump), while reciting a accompanying rhyme. The rhyme could be: 'Dree-dra-drike – how much fruit would you like?' or 'Tra-ree-rare – I am there'. (The meaningless syllables can be replaced with any sound combinations.) The number of squares drawn for the hopscotch has to correspond to the number of words or syllables in the rhyme.

At the end, the dice are thrown (both the number and the fruit dice) and the children are allowed to buy the type and number of fruit indicated by the dice. The fruit seller has pretend fruit made from cardboard, wood, plastic or play dough, or simply a piece of paper onto which different fruit have been drawn with counters placed on each fruit. In the last case, the children get the counters instead of the fruit. This game could be made into a competition: who or which group has the most fruit, or who has got the most fruit of a particular type?

Aims: developing coordination, body control, articulation (particularly of consonant clusters), enjoying talking, understanding of quantity concepts

Materials: chalk, number dice, fruit dice, pretend fruit or a piece of paper and counters

(45) Conker bath

If you have some horse chestnut trees in your neighbourhood, the children can collect enough conkers to fill a small bathtub or paddling pool. If they do this, they can have a conker 'bath' as well as using the conkers for imaginative play, role-play and craft activities. The pressure of the conkers on the body while having a conker 'bath' in them is particularly good for stimulating deep tactile sensations. Conkers also seem to stimulate children's imagination and, because freshly fallen conkers feel so good, they are likely to be a favourite toy for quite a while. Acorns, too, are suitable for bathing, playing and creating things.

Aims: facilitating hand-eye coordination and finger motor skills (while collecting conkers), stimulating deep tactile sensations, developing imagination, fine motor skills (while making things), enjoying talking

---

Materials: lots of conkers or acorns, baby bath or paddling pool

---

46 Dragon skip

Draw a dragon with a long tail with ribbons, either on the floor or on an old sheet. A dice is put on the dragon's head. The children are also given a worksheet each with a picture of a dragon which they colour in as they play. Alternating between straddle jumps and standing jumps for different ribbons, the children jump along to the dragon's head. If they throw a three, for example, they jump along three ribbons to the dragon's head and tell the others, 'I am allowed to colour in three ribbons', then they do this on their worksheets. Who will be first to colour in all their dragon ribbons?

If the jumping works well, the children could accompany the jumps with nonsense syllables (tree-trar-tri; see-sar-so), or even a small rhyme, such as, 'Dragon, dragon, don't fly away, I really, really want you to stay'.

Aims: developing body coordination, articulation of individual sounds during syllable exercises, auditory memory while reciting the rhyme, linking speech and movement

Materials: chalk, an old sheet, a dice, worksheets

Snow angels

For this game, everyone goes out into the snow. If there is a gentle slope nearby, get everyone to stand in front of it; they can simply let themselves fall backwards, landing in the soft snow. If not, everyone will have to be more careful when they let themselves fall, or simply lie down in the snow. Once the children are lying on their backs in the snow, get them to make snow angels. To do this, ask them to move their arms up and down – the tracks in the snow will look like angels' wings. While doing this, everyone could say: 'Arms up – arms down'. Do this several times to make particularly nice wings. Then make the angel's dress, by moving the legs apart and closing them again, using small movements, and, at the same time, lifting the legs a little. While doing this, the children can say: 'Legs apart – legs together', continuing until their legs have left deep tracks in the snow.

Everyone stands up and has a look at their snow angels. Then the children can swap places and try to guess which angel belongs to whom.

The adult starts by saying: 'I was lying next to Michael. What about you?', and walks up to her angel. The next player continues, 'I was lying between Julie and Martin'.

The children then lie down on their angels again, and enjoy the sensation of pretending to be an angel. Perhaps

a snow angel could pretend to take off, and describe what he can see, whom he will meet, and so on. The following day, check whether the snow angels are still there or whether they have flown away.

Aims: developing body awareness, coordination and imagination, practising the concepts up/down, together/apart, next to/between

Materials: snowy landscape

48 The four seasons mime

Everyone agrees mimes to represent the four seasons.

◆ For *spring* crouch down together and then slowly grow upwards.
◆ For *summer*, make swimming movements – stand on one leg and row with the arms and the other leg.
◆ In *autumn* the leaves fall off the trees – stretch your arms out to the side and up, wiggling the fingers, while moving the arms down.
◆ Because *winter* is cold and makes you shiver, give yourself a big, firm hug to keep warm. Pick up on the children's ideas!

Then spread picture cards depicting the four seasons (see Game 18, *The four seasons*, page 43) around the room. While the music is playing, the children walk between the different seasons – when the music stops, the name of a season is called out. The children have to stand next to the corresponding picture card and mime the season. If the children can read letters, the initial letters of the seasons could be used as signals (Sp, S, A, W).

Aims: developing imagination, awareness and understanding of the four seasons, matching pictures to the seasons, developing speed of reaction, visual perception, body awareness

Materials: picture cards of the four seasons – possibly letter cards (Sp, S, A, W)

(49) Anna's day

Form a circle. One child stands in the middle, and starts the game by miming 'getting up'. The children who are watching put the mime into words and say, 'Anna [or Peter] is getting up'. Then the named child, sitting on the floor, is pulled around the room once by their ankles, until they get back to their original place. The next child in the middle of the circle then repeats the first representation and adds another one (for example, 'getting washed'). The children watching verbalise the mime: 'Anna [or Peter] is getting up and getting washed', before taking that child for a ride around the room by their ankles. Then it is the next child's turn to mime 'getting up, getting washed and getting dressed'. Again, the other children verbalise the mime together: 'Anna [or Peter] is getting up, getting washed and getting dressed', and so on, while the sentence gets longer and longer.

You could vary the game in two ways:

◆ The child in the middle of the circle does both – the mime and verbalising the mime.
◆ The child in the middle of the circle gives a verbal instruction and the children in the circle carry out the mime.

Aims: consciously thinking about daily routines, vocabulary development, practising third person verb tense, acting out mimes, memory training, developing proprioception

Materials: none

(50) Nudging balloons

Everyone tries different ways to nudge balloons into the air: with the right/left hand, the head, the shoulder, the knee, the right/left elbow, the right/left index finger. Then two children at a time transport a balloon together to an agreed place in a particular way: between the palms of their hands, between their foreheads, their noses, their upper arms, their bottoms, their tummies, their legs – pick up on the children's ideas. Afterwards, the children can massage each other using the balloons, by rolling the balloon across their bodies while applying a little pressure. Calming music will further facilitate relaxation.

Aims: Improving body perception, naming body parts, developing touch sensation, agility, imagination

Materials: balloons

51 Changing a ball into a line

The children lie down on their tummies on the floor, with arms stretched over their heads and eyes closed. The adult rolls a marble or ball inside a hoop. When the children hear the ball or marble rolling, they say a magic spell: 'Fill, full, fall – I become a ball!' Then they pull their knees forward and under their bodies with their arms, until they each resemble a ball. Once the ball or marble has stopped, they say another magic spell: 'Thunder, lightening, fine – the ball becomes a line!', and, once again, they stretch out their arms and legs, relax and wait with their eyes closed for the ball or marble to start rolling again.

Aims: developing auditory perception, concentration, body awareness, appropriate muscle tension and relaxation, coordination, understanding of the concepts 'ball' and 'line', developing memory, articulation

Materials: ball/marble, hoop

(52) How do animals move?

Discuss with the children how different animals move about. Then ask everyone to try and imitate their movements: a bird flaps its wings, a tiger slinks along, a rabbit hops, a frog jumps, a horse gallops, a monkey climbs, an elephant stomps, a snake slithers, a stork struts, a mouse rushes, a duck waddles, and so on.

Then the adult or one of the children says: 'Flap your wings like …', and the children have to complete the sentence with the name of an animal, in this case, 'a bird', and copy a bird's movements. While the children are moving about, the adult holds up a green signal (for example, a green cardboard disc). As soon as the red signal appears, the children have to stop copying that animal and wait for the next instruction. Afterwards, the children take it in turn to mimic an animal. The other children have to guess what they are and then call out the animal. For example: 'You have been climbing like a monkey!' and so on.

Aims: developing proprioception, expanding vocabulary, developing visual attention

---

Materials: green and red signals (for example, cardboard discs)

---

53 What animal am I?

Prepare some animal picture cards, and a string onto which pretzels have been threaded. First, talk about the individual animals on the cards with the children. Then each child chooses an animal, and the other children have to try and guess which animal each of them has chosen. The children can take it in turn to ask questions, but the 'animal' is only allowed to respond with a nod or a shake of the head. For example, the children might ask: 'Have you got wings? Have you got four legs? Have you got a beak? Do you lay eggs? Do you live in a stable? Do you live in the desert? Can you swim? Do you live in the water? Do you eat grass? Do you live underground?' With every headshake, the 'animal' is allowed to eat one pretzel off the string (without using his hands). With every nod of the head, the child asking the question is allowed to eat a pretzel off the string.

Aims: asking targeted questions, vocabulary development, developing body awareness, oro-motor skills

Materials: animal picture cards, pretzels, string

54 With or without feathers?

For this game you need animal and bird picture cards. You also need to make symbols representing 'with feathers' and 'without feathers', and place these somewhere a little out of the way. The children take it in turn to choose a picture card and say the first syllable of the animal or bird's name. When a child guesses the correct name, he then has to say whether that creature has feathers or not. Then he is allowed to check by looking at the card. If he is correct, he can take the card to the correct symbol.

If the creature has feathers, the child pretends to fly over a raised area (for example, a bench, a mountain made from gym mats, or a box). If the creature does not have feathers, the child has to pull himself along a bench on his tummy.

Afterwards, you could play a memory game. 'Who can remember a creature with or without feathers?' The child who remembers correctly receives that picture card.

Aims: developing proprioception, symbolic understanding, recognising similarities, categorising, developing initial sound recognition, gross motor skills, memory

Materials: paper/cardboard for the symbols, animal and bird picture cards (for example, from an animal pairs game)

55 Aeroplane interviews

Children are interviewed on a pretend aeroplane. Picture cards representing different occupations are spread out. Each child chooses an occupation. Then everyone pretends that they are on an aeroplane (they could use a long bench or line up a row of chairs). The child at the front pretends to be the pilot. The passengers spread out their arms, copying the movements made by the pilot: for example, leaning forward, leaning back, to the left, to the right, and so on.

The adult or another child pretends to be a reporter and interviews the children: 'What is your occupation?', 'What equipment do you need to do your job?', 'Do you work on your own, or with others?', 'What do you have to do?', 'What is your day like?', and 'Where are you flying today?'

This game is particularly good fun for the children if a real recording device is available, and the children can listen to their interviews on the 'radio' afterwards.

Aims: learning about different occupations, developing enjoyment in speaking, body control, appropriate body tension, speed of reaction

Materials: picture cards for the occupations, long bench, a tape recorder (optional)

(56) Builder visit

This game is played in pairs. Each pair agrees on an occupation and how to represent it. The children pretend that they need a plumber (or a doctor, window cleaner, fireman, carpenter). Start the game with a telephone call to the plumber (make a ringing sound) and have a conversation with him. Follow on with a ring at the door bell (make a ding-dong sound) and the greeting at the front door. A description of the work to be carried out and the work itself can be acted out by the pair. At the end of each performance, the other children pull each pair of actors back to their original places (because the performance was so exhausting). For each child, you will need two children or one adult to pull.

Aims: developing enjoyment in speaking, imagination, articulation of individual sounds or sound sequences, consolidating knowledge of different occupational terms, developing proprioception and tactile sensation

Materials: none, but possibly some props to support the role-play

57 Snail shell jumping

A snail is drawn on the floor and divided into squares. In addition, each child is given a piece of paper with a picture of a snail on it. Its shell has also been divided into squares. The child has to jump or hop along the squares and back without touching the lines. Anybody who manages to jump the whole way without touching the lines is allowed to throw a dice and colour in the corresponding number of squares on their snail shell. The game continues until all squares have been coloured in.

If the jumping itself works well, you can accompany the jumps with a rhyme. For the following rhyme you will need 19 squares, which will give you one square for each syllable for a return journey.

Snail, snail, snail,
Don't step on that nail,
Don't pull in your horns,
And mind those prickly thorns.

Aims: developing body control, body coordination, stimulating balance, developing articulation, auditory memory, perception of rhythm, fine motor skills, hand-eye coordination, understanding of quantity

Materials: chalk, dice, worksheets

58 Animals in a spring meadow

Everyone goes for a walk to look at a meadow and observe the animal life. Which creatures can the group spot? In case you are unlucky and there are not many animals to see, you could bring some animal pictures to look at instead.

Take it in turns to ask each other questions about the creatures in the meadow (or in the picture books). For example, one child could start by saying, 'I have seen a creature that can fly and loves to land on beautiful flowers where it collects nectar'. If another child thinks he knows what creature is being described, he asks, 'Are you thinking of a bee?' The first child replies, 'Yes. Now you are all bees!' Then all the children buzz about like bees, until the first child gives a previously agreed signal. At that moment all the 'bees' have to hide immediately from their predator. Discuss who the predator might have been. The children can also talk about their hiding places. Then it is another child's turn to describe an animal for everyone to guess.

Aims: developing visual perception, enjoyment in speaking, verbalising observations, using singular/plural animal names, developing gross motor skills, body awareness, articulation of individual sounds/sound sequences when copying animal sounds, using prepositions

Materials: none, but possibly picture(s) of animals

59 Caterpillar and butterfly

To start with, make flowers by folding or cutting them out of paper. The paper flowers are spread out on the floor, and a very small sweet or tissue-paper ball is placed on each flower. Then everyone pretends to be caterpillars, moving between the flowers. To do this, they lie on their backs and inch along with their heels, alternately pushing their backs down on the floor, then flexing up again. This also helps to tense and relax the bottom and upper thigh muscles. Alternatively, they could lie on their stomachs and move along by alternately lifting their bottoms and their chests. The group moves along like caterpillars until an agreed signal is given; then they fly away as butterflies. The butterflies fly to a flower and drink the nectar by sucking up the sweet or the tissue-paper ball with a straw. They also have to try to remember their flight path and fly back to the start, re-tracing their path.

Aims: developing body awareness, awareness of muscle tension and relaxation, auditory attention, hand-eye control and oro-motor skills, ability to orientate in a room

Materials: paper flowers, tiny sweets or tissue-paper for nectar, plastic straws

(60) Buzz, buzz, buzz!

Cut out paper flowers and write numbers, or draw dice numbers, on the flowers (depending on the developmental stage of the group). The flowers are spread out on the floor around the room. On each flower there is a little bit of nectar (you could use a small building block).

The children are divided into two groups. One child throws a dice and pretends to be a bee flying through the room, spreading his arms and moving them up and down while walking, looking out for the flower with the corresponding number. The bees accompany their 'flight' with the following rhyme:

'Buzz, buzz, buzz – now I am buzzing around. On this flower I will unwind – there, sweet nectar I will find' (or, 'no sweet nectar I will find')'.

While doing this, the child should try not to step on any of the flowers. If he finds a flower with the corresponding number, he lands on this flower, takes the nectar and flies with a '*zzz*' sound back to the group.

Each group uses the building blocks to build a tower. Whose tower is higher? When a child throws a number and there is no nectar on the corresponding flower, he has to buzz home empty-handed.

Aims: developing finger motor skills, understanding of quantity, matching dice pictures to numerals, developing room orientation, body coordination, memory, consolidating the sound *z*

Materials: paper, safety scissors, pencils, building blocks, a dice

61 Frog and stork

One child is the stork and the other children are frogs. The frogs are only allowed to jump like a frog to move along, while making a frog sound, 'ribbit'. The child playing the stork is only allowed to move about on one leg and has to use his outstretched arms to represent the stork's beak opening and closing. The stork says: 'Walk, walk, walk, I am the stork. I'm stalking around the bog and I'm going to catch a frog!' Then he tries to use his beak to catch a frog.

The frog that has been caught turns into a stork. Now there are two storks that say the rhyme together and hunt for frogs.

Aims: developing gross motor skills, coordination, memory, articulation

Materials: none

(**62**) Seals in danger

Everyone pretends to be seals. The children lie down on their tummies in a corner of the room and prop themselves up on their arms. The arms are stretched out and the hands flat on the floor. The children's legs are their tails and are dragged along behind them. The seals play with a ball by knocking it with their heads from one seal to another.

The 'sea witch' tells them that someone is after the seals: hunters are coming. The witch wants to help the seals and tells them of a magic spell which they can use to turn themselves into snakes so that the hunters will be scared of them: 'Whale and shark and witch's knee – now a snake I want to be'.

Two children pretend to be the hunters. One hunter is blindfold. When the seals hear a gunshot (a beat on a drum), they have to recite the magic spell, turn into snakes and slither with a *sss* hiss towards the hunters. The 'seeing' hunter is only allowed to use words to guide the blind hunter towards an agreed haven, otherwise he will be caught by the snakes.

If the snakes catch the blind hunter before he reaches the safe place, he turns into a snake and the snake that has caught him becomes a hunter for the next round. The seals are out of danger, and can turn themselves back

into seals using the following magic spell: 'Whale and shark and witch's knee – a seal again I want to be'. Then the seals can continue their ball game until they hear the hunters approaching again.

Aims: developing body awareness, body control, articulation, verbal memory, acoustic perception, reaction, room orientation, understanding the terms left, right, forwards, backwards, developing trust, consolidating the sound *s*

Materials: ball, drum

(**63**) Mime game

All the children stand or sit in a row facing in the same direction. One child moves forward so that all the others can see him well, demonstrates a body position and describes the movement – everybody else copies the position. Particular attention should be paid to the left and the right side of the body. For some children you may want to mark the right side of the body (using a rubber ring, elastic band, or waterproof pen, etc).

Aims: developing room orientation, body awareness, understanding the terms right/left and different body part names, developing visual perception, imagination

> **Materials:** none; possibly materials for marking, as above

64 My foot is turning in circles

Everyone sits with their feet stretched out in front of them, circling first the right and then the left foot while singing the simple tune: 'My foot is going around in circles, fee, fee, fee – fee, fee, fee, my foot is going around in circles, fee, fee, fee'.

The syllables can be replaced as you like. The feet could also be moved up and down to the tune:

'My foot goes up and my foot goes down, deedle, deedle, dom – deedle, deedle, dom – my foot goes up and my foot goes down, deedle, deedle, dom'.

Aims: developing foot motor skills, body awareness, consolidating sounds in syllables

Materials: none

65 Clever feet

Different objects are placed on the floor. The children are barefoot. They have a good look at the objects and try to memorise them. Then one child closes his eyes, while another child adds an object and puts a cloth over the objects to cover them. The first child then opens his eyes and tries to lift up the cloth using his toes, while the other child recites a little rhyme, such as: 'Spider's leg and witch's brew, which of these things is really new?'

Particularly agile children could also try to catch the cloth with their hands. Then the first child looks at the objects and tries to guess what has been added.

Aims: developing foot and toe motor skills, hand-eye coordination, visual memory, body coordination, articulation, verbal memory

> **Materials:** different objects, cloth (eg scarf, clean tea towel)

(66) Hopscotch

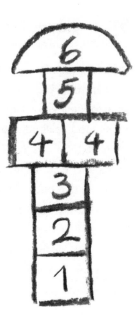

Using chalk, draw hopscotch squares on the floor. Each child is allowed to jump. One syllable is articulated for each square jumped, for example: 'See, saw, sad – I am glad!' or 'What is hiding in the bag?' The nonsense syllables can be varied as much as you like.

Suggested movements for a jump sequence for six squares: squares 1, 2, 3 – one-legged; square 4: straddle vault; squares 5, 6: end jump (turning around while jumping).

If the child manages the jumps while articulating correctly until the end of his turn, he is allowed to reach into a bag and guess an object by feeling it.

Aims: developing gross motor skills, whole body coordination, articulation and consolidation of different sounds in syllables, developing tactile perception

Materials: chalk, bag with a selection of objects for feeling

67 Tower of children

The children get together into small groups of three to five children, and lie on top of each other to build a tower. When there is an earth tremor (fast, quiet knocking on the floor or on a drum), the tower collapses. Each child can, if they like, have a turn at lying right at the bottom and right at the top of the tower. Afterwards, talk about how they felt and what they could feel.

Aims: developing body awareness, tactile perception, body contact, being gentle, concentrating, developing auditory attention, reaction, verbalising feelings

Materials: drum

68 What goes with spring?

The children get together in pairs and sit on the floor, back to back. The adult goes through a list of different phrases, for example, 'daffodils in the gardens'. If the children hear a term that goes with spring, the pairs have to try to push each other away. If the term does not go with spring, they have to remain still.

Other ways of touching may also be used – for example, palms of hands against palms of hands, tummy against tummy, and body side against body side.

Play the game in exactly the same way for the other three seasons (eg, 'leaves falling' for autumn).

Aims: consolidating seasons vocabulary, stimulating body awareness, developing reaction, auditory attention and auditory differentiation

Materials: none

Games for developing a sense of touch and proprioception

69 A bird is landing

Everyone helps to create a bird from (for example) a polystyrene ball and folded paper. The bird should be so light that one can hardly feel its weight.

Then the children lie on the floor with their eyes closed. Exerting very light pressure, the adult touches each child with the bird three times in a row on different parts of the body, and asks: 'Tweet, tweet, tweet, where is the bird?' The child has to remember the last touch and, still with his eyes closed, describe the position of the bird. Then the child is allowed to open their eyes and check whether they are right. One of the children can then be asked to try the bird on his friends – this will facilitate body parts awareness and articulation.

Variation

Ask the children to try to recall the first two points of touch. Alternatively, the adult can touch the child on the same place three times in a row – depending on the child's stage of development.

Materials: polystyrene ball, paper

---

70 Will the door to the magic castle open?

You will need a set of objects beginning with the sound you would like to target. The objects are hidden under a cloth and can only be guessed and named by feeling them under the cloth, using hands or feet. All objects have to be taken to the 'magic castle' individually by the children. However, the castle gate will only open if a particular object is taken along the path to the castle in a particular way (for example, with the elbow joint, the knee joint, between ear and shoulder, between chin and neck, under the armpit, between the upper thighs).

In addition, a specific sequence of knocks could be agreed that needs to be used to open the castle gate. When the gate to the castle opens, the magician (a puppet or finger puppet) tells the child who has knocked a short magical story or shows him a magical trick.

> **Materials:** objects which begin with the sound you want to practise, cloth to cover them

71 An annoying fly

The children sit with closed eyes and the adult touches each child in turn with cotton wool or a feather somewhere around the face. The child who has been touched then indicates where the 'fly' landed by saying, 'The fly sat on my nose', and so on.

If you are working with a child who is tactilely defensive, it is better to use a cotton bud or little stick which has a wooden bead attached to its end rather than cotton wool, because being touched with cotton wool or a feather could be uncomfortable for these children.

> **Materials:** cotton bud, wooden bead, feather, cotton wool

72 Hands tower

The children work in groups of twos or threes. One child puts a flat hand on the table while another puts one hand on top, and so on until all hands are building a tower. Then the hand at the bottom is pulled out and placed on top again. The next hand follows suit and the pace becomes faster and faster until the hands tower collapses. While doing this, repeatedly recite syllables or little rhymes.

> **Materials:** none

73 Visit to the little witch

In order to visit the little witch, the children have to move along a prescribed route laid out by 'stones' (circles that have been marked on the floor by the group using chalk or carpet tiles). For added fun, the children have to move along the stones on all fours.

Once arrived at the witch's place, the children can recite spells such as 'Hax – hex – hix: three and three makes six'. You could also make up a delicious witch-like recipe:

'Stirry, goody, slobberdash, ready is the mouse mash' (or spider mash, beetle mash, larva mash, slug mash).

'Glug, glug, stir, make, ready is the ant cake' (or mouse cake, fly cake, worm cake).

'Hocus-pocus what a treat, spiders' feet are what I eat.'

'Hocus-pocus apple core, frogspawn pudding – give me more!'

'Hocus-pocus peach and plum, rats' tails are so yummy – yum!', and so on.

Variation

If the 'stones' marking the path to the little witch also have different colours, for example, two blue 'stones' (two carpet tiles, or similar) for the hands and two red ones for the feet, the task becomes more difficult: the hands are now only allowed to touch blue 'stones' and the feet are only allowed to touch red 'stones'.

Materials: chalk or carpet tiles

74) Massage guessing game

The children lie on the floor with their eyes closed and the adult rubs the arms and/or legs of each child in turn, using different materials. After a child has experienced being rubbed with two different materials, he opens his eyes and points out the two that have been used by the adult from a choice of several materials.

While doing this the child says, 'You have washed me with …', or 'You have rubbed me with …'

Materials: could include a flannel, massage glove, sponge, back-scrubbing brush, nailbrush

75 Cribbel-crabbel-crag – what is in the bag?

Together with the children fill little 'feely' bags (fabric bags or pillow covers that are tied with ribbons or string) with different things. You could use natural materials such as stones, fir cones, acorns, beechnuts, chestnuts, wooden discs, sand, rice, sunflower seeds, beans and so on, or even toys. The therapeutic value of this game is increased greatly if we collect the materials together with the children.

Now everyone says a magic spell and feels the outside of the bags with their fingers or toes to determine what is inside. The magic spells can be changed depending on the sound to be practised:

'Simsalabimbambad – what is in the bag?'
'Shi-sho-shack – what is in the sack?'
'Shribbel-shrabbel-schrack – what is in the sack?'
'Bri-bro-brack – what is in the sack?'
'Tri-tro-track – what is in the sack?'
'Fri-fro-frack – what is in the sack?', and so on.

After the spell has been cast, the bag can be opened to check its contents. You might like to get a few children to feel the contents of the bag with closed eyes before opening their eyes to see if the spell has worked. Then the bags are tied up again.

Variations

The game can also be played without a magic spell. Instead, a repetitive sentence structure containing a target sound is chosen. For example, if one wants to practise the S or K in a sentence, say 'There are … in the sack'; if one wants to practise F in a sentence, say 'I can feel …'

Another variation is to fill two bags at a time with the same material. The children then have to find two bags containing the same materials. In this way, a tactile pairs game can be played.

Materials: fabric bags or pillow covers, ribbons or string. Stones, fir cones, acorns, beechnuts, chestnuts, wooden discs, sand, rice, sunflower seeds, beans, even toys.

---

76 Enchanted water

Objects containing the sound to be practised are hidden in a 'feely box' (a box which is covered with a cloth), or a 'feely bag'. Picture cards with representations of these items are lined up to the left and right of a piece of rope stretched along the floor. Now the children have to feel the objects in the 'feely box', label them, carry them to the matching picture card and place them there. However, on the way there each child has to balance on the rope because next to the rope there is 'magic water'. If the children fall into the water, they turn into 'earthworms' and have to crawl through the soil. This could involve them crawling through a big tunnel made from piled-up gym mats, or crawling along underneath a large blanket.

Materials: 'feely' box or bag, picture cards depicting objects in the bag, rope, gym mats or large blanket.

77 Magic fairy stones

The children lie on the floor with their eyes shut and the fairy touches them with her magic wand. Each child has to indicate exactly where he has been touched, and name the corresponding body part. If the child has felt correctly, the fairy places a magic stone into a basket. When the whole group has felt correctly ten times, and the fairy has placed ten stones in the basket, an aromatic treasure chest opens. Each child can choose a favourite smell from the chest, and borrows it to smell or even sample (for this you could fill film containers with different spices, herbs, fruit or vegetable pieces).

Variation

The game can be made more difficult by having the fairy touch the children with different materials. They then have to guess what these are.

> **Materials:** chest (or something with a lid), wand, 10 stones, small containers of different spices, fruit, vegetables

78 The miracle tree

The children stand with their arms spread out and their eyes closed, pretending to be miracle trees from the land of milk and honey, on which different fruit and objects are growing. The adult then touches them in turn somewhere on their bodies. The child who has just been touched indicates where he has been touched, and what is growing in that place on the tree.

Materials: none

79 My body – a fantastic road

The children lie on the floor with their eyes closed (first on their backs and then on their fronts), pretending to be a road. The adult 'drives' along the road (the chain of children) using different 'vehicles' (toy car, large physiotherapy ball, tennis ball, small gymnastic ball, roll, wooden brick, bottle, etc). The children are then asked to say which 'vehicle' has been using their road: for example, 'I could feel a tennis ball drive along my road'.

Materials: toy car, large physiotherapy ball, tennis ball, small gymnastic ball, roll, wooden brick, bottle

80 Did you feel the mouse?

With his eyes closed, each child rolls lengthways along a blanket (representing soil) under which there are many mice (corks that have been cut lengthways). When the child who is rolling feels a mouse, he needs to indicate where he has felt it and say: 'I have felt a mouse on … [my tummy]'.

Materials: blanket, corks

81 Where have the diamonds been hidden?

A burglar has stolen the princess's diamonds. He has buried them in the sand so no one can find them. A puppet tells the story to the group and everyone helps to look for the diamonds. Bury round stones or glass pebbles in a box filled with sand and ask the children to find them by touch.

When the group has found all the diamonds, they return them to the princess. The burglar won't be pleased when he tries to dig up the stolen diamonds.

Instead of diamonds the story could also revolve around magic seeds. For this, bury dried beans or peas.

> **Materials:** box of sand, round stones, glass pebbles, dried beans or peas

82) A journey along the 'feely' road

Use different materials to create stopping points on a 'feely' road before the children set out on their travels. Materials can be placed at the various stopping points to represent natural features (see *Materials*).

Once the materials are in place (see list below) the adult tells a story, which the children act out in mime as they walk along the 'feely' road. The story could be as follows:

We get up first thing in the morning and crawl out of our tents. We close the zip of the tent behind us, *ssst, ssst,* have a wash and listen to the water running, *shshsh.* Then we dry ourselves and head for the beach. To get there we have to go through the forest. The seawater is still a bit cold, so we decide to play on the beach. We look for the biggest and the smallest pebble. We make shapes using the pebbles and create a circle, a square, a triangle or even a little person. We even manage to build a small tower using the pebbles.

Alternatively, you could make up a game.

We try and hit the biggest stone with the smallest one. Meanwhile the water has warmed up. We dive and swim (using mime) to the bridge. The bridge straddles deep water. We stop swimming and climb up onto the bridge, balancing across it. Fish come up close to the bridge. We

can stroke them with our toes and feel their scales. At the end of the bridge on the other side of the water are some boats, which we can use to get to the islands (try putting one foot at a time on a small log and rolling it backwards and forwards). While we are on the boat we sing a suitable song such as, 'When I was young I sucked my thumb, the day I went to sea'.

When we reach the islands, we jump from one island to the next until we have reached the mountains. We climb up and try to stand on one leg on top of a mountain. Behind the mountains we find our beach again. It is now nearly lunchtime, and we have to be back in time for lunch.

Materials:	
bark and moss	a forest
pebbles of different sizes	a beach
two small wooden logs	a boat
(about 20cm long and 10cm wide)	
a rope	a bridge
fir cones	fish
bigger flat stones	islands
large wooden blocks	mountains

(83) Lots of worms!

The children can use play dough to make lots of worms of different lengths and thicknesses. Then everyone hides all the worms under a cloth (soil). The children now have to try and find the longest (shortest, fattest, thinnest) worm. Afterwards, they can sort the worms according to different criteria and everyone can practise saying: 'This is the longest worm', and so on.

Variation
You can also make balls, snakes, moons, sticks, or similar objects and feel for, or sort, by different criteria.

Materials: play dough, cloth

84 Guessing game on the 'feely' road

The adult builds a 'feely' road together with the children. To make the road, use A4 or A5 cardboard sheets and smaller pieces of different materials (plastic, sandpaper, carpet tiles, synthetic fur, cork, wood, aluminium foil, clear plastic plates, ceramic tiles, mesh, sheep wool, hessian, etc). Stick the pieces of material onto the cardboard, and line them up on the floor to create a road.

The children then walk along the road barefoot with their eyes closed (or crawl across the road and feel with their hands) and, as they walk, they are given different instructions, such as 'Walk along to the fur!', or 'Tell me what you are standing on at the moment!' The pieces of cardboard are swapped around intermittently. You could ask the child who is walking on the road to try to remember the order of materials that appear on the pieces of cardboard and to predict which one comes next. The child is then in control of checking himself by feeling with his foot whether or not his prediction has been correct.

Variation
The game can be varied by 'changing' one or several pieces of cardboard. For example, the piece of fur could be an animal that the children are going to visit and feed. The tile could be a swimming pool that the children

could pretend to swim on by making swimming movements – they could even try to stand on the tile on one leg. The clear plastic plate could become a window through which they can see different things. The piece of plastic could be a shopping bag. The children can tell each other all the things that they have bought while they are standing on it. The carpet tile could be a magic carpet, which they can use to fly away on and experience different adventures. The aluminium foil could be an astronaut's suit, which children could use to walk on the moon, in slow motion. The piece of hessian could be a potato sack which tells us stories about things it has experienced, and so on.

Materials: objects for a 'feely' road: plastic, sandpaper, carpet tiles, synthetic fur, cork, wood, aluminium foil, clear plastic plates, ceramic tiles, mesh, sheep wool, hessian, A4 or A5 cardboard sheets.

85 Touch the pairs

Stick identical materials onto two pieces of card at a time. Either the children have to feel for two identical pieces of card with their eyes closed or they are blindfold and given a card, and then they have to find the second one on the floor. During this game, a range of opportunities for talking is created as the children discuss the texture and qualities of different materials.

Materials: card with textured material

86 The dwarf at the mountain

Ask each child to try and build a tower with building blocks, or complete a pegboard while blindfold. If the child succeeds, the dwarf comes out of his mountain cave and plays with him. The mountain cave could be made from papier mâché, clay or wood. A simpler solution would be for the adult to use her fist for a mountain cave and her little finger for the dwarf.

The child's developmental stage will determine how many attempts each child can have to build the tower or complete the pegboard. If the child has built the tower from different coloured building blocks he can then draw a copy of the tower.

Materials: building blocks, pegboard, mountain cave (papier mache, clay or wood)

87 The busy donkey

Each child pretends to be a donkey and walks on all fours. The adult loads up the donkey with different materials. The donkey has to guess what is on his back and take the load to an agreed destination. While doing this the child tells everyone what he is carrying. For example: 'I am carrying a beanbag, a toy brick, a cushion, a gym ball', etc, or 'I am a donkey and I carry a heavy load. It's a cushion, and I can't keep going any more'. Of course the donkey receives some food for his hard work: for example, a Twiglet or breadstick, which he is only allowed to pick up with his lips (without using his hands to help).

> **Materials:** beanbag, toy brick, cushion, gym ball, Twiglets or breadsticks

88 Through the magic forest

In this game, the children have to get through the magic forest to the king's castle without stumbling. A knight is waiting in the castle. He needs their help. The forest is very dark. Each child closes their eyes and is led through the forest undergrowth (lots of strings hung from the ceiling and wound around furniture). The child has to climb over all these strings 'blindly'. At the castle the king and the knight are waiting for him with a big task. There is a quest to free the princess, who has been kidnapped by a robber. Together, all the children plan how to rescue her. Perhaps they could try and trick the robber away from his house by making a noise for him to investigate?

Materials: string, objects to create a forest

(89) Garden work

Before the children can work in the garden, they need to carry different tools there. They can take turns to be the wheelbarrow which is then loaded up by the adult with all the different tools (picture cards, which the children have cut out of an old catalogue), and then 'pushed' to the garden. To mimic pushing the wheelbarrow, the child walks on his hands and the adult holds the child up by their upper thighs.

Whilst the wheelbarrow is moving the rest of the group say, 'We are taking the hose to the garden' or, 'We need the spade in the garden'. Then the children can take it in turns to mime the different garden activities (digging, raking, planting, and so on) while the others try to guess which tool is required by naming it or pointing to it.

Variation
The garden tools can also be transported in a handcart. To do this, the child sits on the floor and the adult pulls the child along by their feet.

Materials: cut out pictures of garden tools

90) **What floats?**

Place different things (wood, stone, eraser, pencil, paper boat, plastic boat, coin, leaf, cork, pencil sharpener, spoon, button, cup etc) in a 'feely' box or bag. The children can feel them by using either their hands or feet, and name the different items, ideally using a whole sentence.

The children then guess whether or not the different objects will float on water. Objects are sorted according to 'will float' and 'will not float', then the child can try out the different objects in a bowl or a basin full of water. The children can talk about their observations: 'The stone does not float on water [lake, stream, river, pond, puddle]', or 'The wood floats on water', and so on.

> **Materials:** wood, stone, eraser, pencil, paper boat, plastic boat, coin, leaf, cork pencil sharpener, spoon, button, cup, bowl

91) We want to go swimming

The items that are needed to go swimming are placed in a 'feely' box, or under a cloth. The children guess what the different objects are (beach towel, hand towel, sun lotion, inflatable ring, arm bands, inflatable animal, water ball, sun hat, sunglasses, swimsuits, flippers, snorkel, goggles) by feeling with their hands or feet. They then name them and explain what they are used for. Then the group enacts different scenarios associated with going swimming, using role-play: paying to get into the pool; putting sun lotion on each other; squirting each other with water; swimming; playing with the ball, and so on.

After this, the children could decorate a cotton swimming bag using fabric paints. The swimming things are packed, and the children are asked to remember all the things they have put in their bags: 'I packed my swimming bag and I put in…' The adult takes out the things that each child has named. At the end, the children can keep the bags which they have decorated.

> **Materials:** cloth or 'feely' box, beach towel, swimsuit, armbands, sunhat, sun lotion, sunglasses, snorkel, goggles, flippers, inflatable animal, water ball. Cotton bags, fabric paint (both optional)

92 Goal!

Several goal posts are cut out of a wide piece of cardboard. Each child is given a selection of objects that begin with a target sound. He is then allowed to feel the objects with his hands or feet, keeping his eyes closed in order to guess and name them.

Each object has a corresponding picture card, which is placed in or above one of the goals. Each child tries to shoot or roll a ball into the goal containing the picture card that corresponds to his object. If the child hits the goal, he is allowed to keep the picture card.

If no picture cards are available the objects could be numbered. The goals should also be numbered, and the child has to aim for the goal with the number matching their object.

Materials: cardboard (for goal posts), picture cards, ball

93 Traffic jam

There is a traffic jam on the road: the children line up lots of cars in a row. Some cars are pointing to the right, some to the left. Each child closes his eyes and has to identify by touch all the cars pointing to the left (or right). While doing this he says, 'This car is going right/left'. Make an arrow out of sandpaper and stick it on a piece of card to give the child some extra help in working out the direction.

Afterwards the children can play cars. They can pretend to be stuck in a traffic jam, or they can invent stories about where different drivers are planning to go.

Materials: toy cars, sandpaper, arrow

94 Can you feel the conker? (2)

Put lots of different things, such as conkers, acorns, fir cones, nuts, marbles, wooden beads, stones, pebbles etc, in a 'feely' bag. Depending on the sound to be targeted, the children are asked to pick a specific item. The child who picks out the object talks about what he is doing: 'This is a nut, too', or 'I can feel another conker'.

Materials: conkers, acorns, fir cones, nuts, marbles, wooden beads, stones, pebbles

95 Shopping game

First, put everything needed to set up shop into a box. The children take turns to guess the objects by feeling them, then they name them and sort them out for the 'shop'. Then the adult and the children make bags and write price labels. The adult then 'buys' some things in the newly created shop. The children carefully fill the bags with conkers, fruit and other items. All the children's actions are verbalised, so each child and the adult will have the opportunity for many verbal exchanges.

It is even more fun if, prior to this activity, the adult and the children prepare items for the shop such as shaped and painted fruit, vegetables, sweets, biscuits, cakes, sausages and cheese, using play dough.

Materials: box, sticky labels, pens, shop goods (conkers, fruit, etc)

96   Mouse or bear?

Compile different pictures of mice and bears (or of one big, heavy animal and one small, light animal) in different situations. The children should sit or stand in a circle. From behind, the adult lightly or heavily leans onto the shoulders of each child. The child has to guess what the animal is. For example, 'You are the bear [the mouse]!'

After this game, the children take a card from the 'bear pile' or the 'mouse pile' and, one by one, talk about what the bear or mouse is doing. Everyone pretends to be either bears or mice and tries to copy the situations. Then everyone swaps roles. If you don't have any pictures the children can simply use their imagination. The person who is pretending to be the animal can demonstrate a bear or mouse movement, and another person can try to copy them. Alternatively, the animal could talk about itself, or the child could recite one of the following examples:

Bear: Grrr, grrr, grrr – I'm covered in fur!
        I am a cuddly bear, who's dancing happily here and there.
        But if I hear a sound, I'm going to fall down.

Mouse: Here comes a mouse.
        Dingdong, dingdong.
        Is anyone in the house?

Materials: pictures of mice and bears (or other large/small animals)

97 Counting-out rhyme

A counting-out rhyme, such as 'one potato, two potato' or 'ibble obble, black bobble', is counted out on the fingers of each child in turn. The child who is playing is blindfold and has to indicate the finger that has been touched last, and then bend that finger to hide it. The game continues until only one finger is left. The game could also continue by counting fingers back in and massaging them at the same time.

The children could all say the rhyme together while the adult does the necessary finger movement.

> **Materials:** blindfold

98 Finger puppets

The children's fingers are turned into different animals or characters by wearing finger puppets. The adult could invent a script. When a particular puppet speaks, the child wearing that puppet moves the corresponding finger. It is best to start with one finger puppet per child, but later the children can wear more than one puppet each.

Instead of using finger puppets, you could simply draw on the children's fingers.

> **Materials:** finger puppets or pens

99 Kissing fingers

This game requires fine-motor skills. Everyone sticks red stickers on the tips of their fingers. The stickers represent lips. Now all the fingers line up – the children should spread them wide apart – and take it in turns to kiss the thumb. The fingers have little conversations with the thumb and wave at him to say goodbye.

> **Materials:** red stickers

Tickling game

The children sit or lie with their eyes closed and the adult recites the following rhymes:

'Tickle, tickle, tinger – I am going to tickle your finger'; or

'Tickle, tickle, toot – I am going to tickle your foot'; or

'Tickle, tickle, tose – I am going to tickle your nose', and so on.

After each verse, tickle the named body part on the children. After a while, they are likely to be able to guess, and will name the body part themselves before you have finished the rhyme.

> **Materials:** none

Dinosaur game

The children cut out large dinosaurs from pieces of cardboard. The dinosaurs are given spikes on their backs in the form of clothes pegs. Each child has to put these on with their eyes closed. Now the children can discuss what the dinosaur looks like. What does he eat? Where does he want to go? Where does he sleep? Maybe he needs a friend?

Materials: cardboard, safety scissors, clothes pegs

Shapes on the back

Stick shapes cut from sandpaper onto cardboard. Each child uses his fingertips and later his toes to feel and guess a shape. He then turns over the card and, using his fingers, draws the shape on the back of the person next to him, who has to guess the shape. Check whether the children have got it right by asking them to turn over and look at the pieces of card. Make sure you ask the children to swap roles!

Materials: sandpaper, cardboard, safety scissors

(103) Magic trail

Use liquid glue to paint almost invisible magic trails onto paper: simple shapes such as a circle, a triangle, a square, a house or a cloud are ideal. Ask the children to close their eyes. Hand out the paper and ask the children to feel the magic trail with their fingertips then guess what the shape is. When they have done this, collect the paper, get the children to close their eyes again, and redistribute the shapes.

Materials: liquid glue, paper, safety scissors

Part 2: Balancing games

Balance is the most important sense for dealing with different sensations. It therefore makes an important contribution to the development of receptive and expressive language. It seems that the brain requires a certain degree of balance stimulation in order to form speech sounds, and that sometimes the movement experienced during daily routines is not sufficient to meet this requirement. A close neural link exists between the balance (or vestibular) system and the sense of hearing; the nerve connections from the ear to the brainstem are linked with those of the vestibular system.

Very often, children with speech and language difficulties have difficulties with motor planning and execution. It is therefore important to provide them with strong movement stimuli such as jumping and swinging. The following games involve jumping, spinning, swinging, rocking and driving, and aim to stimulate the vestibular system.

(104) Swap with me!

The children stand in a circle. On the floor there are four beer mats, newspaper pages or toy bricks – these represent rocks breaking the surface of a lake (the floor). Everyone stands on the shore of the lake, wanting to swap places with those on the other side. One child starts the game by calling across the lake:

'Eve, please swap places with me!'

Then both children are spun around in circles by their neighbours, while all the children count to 10 together. The two children are then allowed to cross the lake but they are only allowed to step on the beer mats (toy bricks, newspaper pages).

Aims: consolidating children's names, developing social interaction, stimulating balance, developing body control, articulation

Materials: beer mats, newspaper or big bricks

(**105**) The pirate's treasure

The children close their eyes while picture cards are half-hidden around the room. Each card has a picture of a different container (suitcase, bottle, barrel, trunk, bag, basket, sack, box, jug, pot, rucksack, etc), which is either full or empty.

With the children, build a ship from a soft mat or hammock and pretend to cross the sea as pirates. When a pirate discovers one of the hidden cards (treasure), he jumps out of the boat and swims to fetch it, then tells everybody what he has found and whether the container is full or empty.

If a scooter or skateboard is available, this can be used as a rowing boat into which the pirate climbs from the big ship in order to row to the treasure.

Aims: developing visual perception, stimulating sense of balance, agility, practising the terms full/empty

Materials: mat or hammock for the ship, a scooter or skateboard (optional), picture cards

Wind, storm, thunder and lightning

Different signs are used for wind, storm, thunder and lightning:

◆ *Wind* – waving one or two hands slowly up and down
◆ *Storm* – waving the whole arm about
◆ *Lightning* – drawing a lightning bolt in the air
◆ *Thunder* – drum beat

Begin to play through the game in sequence.

◆ While the adult makes the sign for *wind*, the children have to stand on one leg and flap their arms like birds while articulating an *sss* sound.
◆ If the sign for *storm* is given, the children have to get together in pairs, link hands and spin each other around in a circle, while articulating a *shshsh* sound.
◆ When the signs for *thunder* and *lightning* are given, the children let go and have to freeze in the next position, as if they have been hit by lightning.
◆ Once the sign for *wind* is given again, everybody starts to fly and make the *sss* sound, as before.

The children can then take turns to give the weather signals.

Aims: developing reaction, visual perception, auditory perception, switching from one movement to another, stimulating sense of balance, developing body control, appropriate muscle tension, articulating *sss* and *shshsh*

Materials: drum

Snow mountain

The whole group helps to shovel a large, soft mountain of snow in front of the swing. One child sits on the swing and listens to different spoken words. When hearing a specific signal word, the child has to jump off the swing with a loud yell and land in the snow mountain.

Aims: stimulating sense of balance, developing auditory attention, reaction, and also a little test of courage

Materials: snow, shovel

(108) Find your snowman twin

The children draw lots of pictures of different snowmen, making sure that each picture of a snowman has an identical twin (just like a pairs game). One snowman from each twin pair is put on a pile, and their corresponding partners are spread out at the other end of the room. In addition, there are obstacles around the room.

Each child takes a snowman from the pile and says to it: 'Come along. Let's look for your twin'. Then the child lies on his tummy on a skateboard, makes his way through the obstacles and, at the other end, tries to find the matching snowman. Once he has found the correct snowman, the child says: 'These two snowmen look the same', puts the two cards together and, still on the skateboard, goes back the way he came.

When all the twins have been found, the cards can be shuffled and used to play a pairs game. While playing, the children can practise saying: 'These two snowmen look the same/don't look the same'.

To vary the game, one set of snowmen could be distributed on mats arranged around the outside of a trampoline. The child takes a snowman from the pile and has to jump in circles on the trampoline until he has discovered the snowman twin, at which point he can jump onto the mat.

Aims: developing articulation, stimulating balance, developing visual perception, visual memory

Materials: snowmen picture cards (pairs), skateboard or trampoline and mats

(109) Television interview

First make a television, using an old box. The adult starts by sitting behind the television and talking about the events of her day. Then each child in turn travels to a television interview by car (skateboard or blanket, on which the child is pulled by the other children). The child whose turn it is sits behind the home-made television and the other children pretend to watch. The child answers interview questions, such as: 'What is your day like?' or 'What do you do in the morning, at lunchtime, in the afternoon, and in the evening?'

Aims: stimulating sense of balance, differentiating and naming different times of the day, becoming more aware of daily routines, enjoying talking

Materials: big box, pens, safety scissors or knife, skateboard or blanket

(110) Balloons with content

The children get together in pairs. Each pair is given a balloon, which contains a picture or a word card. One pair starts the game, with one of the children holding the balloon from an elevated position – their partner has to catch the balloon, tie it to his ankle and turn around in circles. The other child climbs down and tries to make the balloon burst by jumping on it. Once the balloon has burst, the pair look at their picture or word card and try to describe the word to the other children without saying it. The other children have to guess the word.

Aims: developing hand-eye control, vestibular stimulation, developing agility, describing items, expanding vocabulary

Materials: balloons, string, picture or word cards

Planet of lies

Pictures or drawings of things that do not correspond to reality can be a great way of encouraging discussion. For this activity, you can use ready-made pictures, asking the children to guess what does not correspond to reality and to explain why something looks wrong, or the children can draw their own pictures, for example: a fish on a lead; a toothbrush in the chimney; a door on a roof; apples and pears on the same tree; a ship on the road; a train on waves; upside-down flowers; a crocodile on a chain outside a dog kennel.

The children are allowed to take it in turns to travel to the planet of lies by rocket. To do this, the child sits on a swing which is pulled back and released at the 'push of a button'. This starts off the engine noise of the rocket (sounds such as *br*, *r*, *cr*, *s* and *sh* can be used to support this). After landing, the child identifies which things exist on the planet of lies that we do not find on our planet.

Afterwards the children can all draw some 'lying pictures' and look at them, one at a time, explaining why certain things are silly or unrealistic.

Aims: vestibular stimulation, enjoying talking, developing logical thinking, visual perception, imagination

Materials: 'silly pictures', paper and pens for drawing, swing

(112) What has changed?

A child changes something about his appearance behind a screen or outside the door, and the others have to guess what has changed. The child lies on his tummy on a skateboard and turns himself in circles by moving the board, while saying:

'What is different, think well. Right or wrong only the light will tell'.

Then he stands up, is given a torch, and switches it on when any of the children guess correctly.

Aims: developing sense of balance, visual attention, visual memory, articulation, finger motor skills

Materials: skateboard, torch

113 All the animals are hungry

Create picture cards of different animals (for example, cow, rabbit, stork, cat, dog, mouse, hen, squirrel, monkey, bear) and picture cards of things the animals like to eat (grass, carrots, frogs, mice, sausages, cheese, grains, nuts, bananas, honey). The animal cards are put in a pile, and the food cards are spread out on the floor at the other end of the room.

One child begins by taking an animal card and then stretches out lengthwise on the floor, rolling over until he gets to the food cards, then choosing the matching food item and telling the other children: 'A cow eats grass'.

The children now discuss whether this is true or not. If they think that the child is correct, they give the following signal: clap their hands twice, slap their upper thighs once, pat the floor once. If they think the answer is wrong, they put their hands in front of their mouths.

If the children signal that they think the answer is correct, the child puts the two cards together by placing the food card underneath the animal card, rolls back into his place, and then it is the next child's turn. If the second signal (for a wrong answer) is given, the child has to choose another food item and is only allowed to roll back into his place when the children give the 'correct' signal.

Eventually, all the food cards should be hidden underneath the animal cards. The children now need to guess what the animals like to eat. They ask each other questions, such as, 'Martin, what does a rabbit eat?' and so on. Then the cards are swapped around and the questioner changes tack, asking, 'Who likes to eat grass?' The children can check whether they are correct by uncovering the cards.

The animal and food cards can also be used to play a pairs game. All the cards are spread face down on the floor. The child whose turn it is uncovers two cards and explains: 'A cow does not like to eat sausages'. Whoever finds two matching cards is allowed to keep them.

Aims: stimulating sense of balance, consolidating use of 'not' and the article 'a', reacting in response to given signals, memory training, developing visual and rhythmical memory

Materials: picture cards of animals and animal food items (in pairs)

114 Occupations game

One half of the picture cards shows people in different occupations, while the other half shows the tools required for them to do their different jobs. Pretend that it is early in the morning, and people want to start working. This is when they notice that they cannot find their tools. A witch passing overhead calls out to them: 'Ha, you are looking for your tools – I have put a spell on them – I don't want people to work. Ha, ha, ha'.

Everyone visits the wizard and asks for his help. The wizard looks in his magic book and tells us that the witch has thrown all the tools in the big witches' lake and turned them into stones. The counter-spell is: 'Wiz, wiz, wiz, stone from a pool, now turn yourself back into a tool'. The wizard also points out the dangers of the witches' lake. No one is allowed to touch the water with their feet. Anybody touching the water will turn into a stone themselves.

The children are allowed to use different materials to build a bridge. They can also build ships. One at a time, the children have to walk across the bridge, or get into a ship, without touching the water. Every time a child says the counter-spell, they are allowed to take a picture card (if a paper clip is attached to each picture card, the children can fish for the cards with a magnetic fishing rod). Then the picture card is matched up with the

correct person and the child explains: 'The cook needs a wooden spoon' or 'The microscope belongs to the scientist', until all the people have got their tools. If a child touches the witches' water with his foot, he turns into a stone. This means he has to lie on the floor and is rolled over to one side by the other children. Of course, in the end the spell is lifted from all of the children.

Aims: vocabulary development, developing articulation, balance, body awareness, imagination, hand-eye coordination (when fishing with a magnetic rod)

> **Materials:** picture pairs (occupations and tools), materials for bridge or ships, paper clips and magnetic rods (optional)

115 Guessing occupations

Use the card pairs from the 'Occupations game' (picture cards depicting different occupations, and picture cards depicting matching tools). One child starts the game by choosing a profession. He then has to look for the matching tool or piece of equipment, after which he places both picture cards face down on the floor so that the other children cannot see them.

The child then sits inside a box (placed on a blanket so it can be pulled along more easily) and makes a hand gesture related to the occupation. One of the other children begins by asking a specific question about the occupation which can only be answered with 'yes' or 'no'. If the answer is 'no', the child who has been asking the question has to pull the child in the box around the room once and then it is the next child's turn to ask a question. If the answer is 'yes', the child is allowed to ask another question. This continues until the occupation has been guessed. Once the occupation has been guessed, check whether the correct tool has been chosen. If the child has chosen the correct tool, he is pulled around the room for a bonus round – if he was wrong, he forfeits the bonus round.

Aims: learning about different professions, vocabulary development, learning to focus questioning, stimulating balance, developing proprioception

Materials: picture card pairs of different occupations and tools, box, blanket

My favourite colour

One child lies in a hammock or sits on a swing. Underneath the hammock or swing is a basket or a flat box containing colourful objects. While swinging gently, the child recites the following verse:

Red, red, red's my favourite colour,
Red, red, as bright as it can be.
Now I'm looking in my basket
How many red things can I see?

The child then takes all the red things out of the basket. To finish, he has to close his eyes and recall which things were red. The next child chooses a different colour. It makes sense to put all the objects back after each round, to ensure there are enough objects from which to select.

Aims: naming and relating colours, developing hand-eye coordination, reaction, articulation, auditory memory, visual memory, stimulating sense of balance

Materials: hammock or swing, a selection of objects in different colours, basket or flat box

117 Looking for signs of spring

Everyone goes for a spring walk and each child calls out when he spots a sign of spring. The children name the signs and take pictures of them. Then they use the photographs to make jigsaw puzzles and spread the pieces out around a trampoline or a mat.

Each child is allowed to jump ten times on the trampoline or mat while turning in circles. Then he stops and chooses a puzzle piece. After choosing each piece, the children guess what it is. In this way they repeat the signs of spring and recall them to memory.

Aims: naming the signs of spring, developing visual perception and attention, vocabulary, stimulating sense of balance

Materials: camera, film, safety scissors, trampoline or thick mat

(118) Games on a spring meadow

On one side of the stream it is still winter – on the other side spring will begin if the correct spell is said:

> Winter, winter, you're not here to stay!
> Sunshine for the flowers can't be far away.
> Abracadabra, magical trick,
> Spring come along now – quick, quick, quick!

One child recites the spell and jumps across the stream. The width of the stream can vary to accommodate the abilities of different children. Once he has arrived on the other side, the child demonstrates what can be done on the spring meadow. The others verbalise the activity (for example, 'Andrew is jumping'), then they jump over to join in. At a signal, the spell is over, and all the children have to cross the stream again to the winter side where spring has to be conjured up once more.

Aims: developing imagination, stimulating the vestibular system, developing articulation, verbal memory, gross motor skills, vocabulary

Materials: chalk or string to mark out the stream

(119) Roundabout game

First of all get the children to make a lookout post (possibly out of cushions or mats). Then the children pretend they are in a playground, riding on a roundabout. To do this they can sit on their bottoms, bend their legs slightly while lifting them off the floor, and use their arms to push themselves around in circles, like spinning tops. They could also try spinning while kneeling and lifting their feet up. While spinning around, they all say:

> On my bottom [knees, etc] I spin around
> Hear me make a joyful sound.
> Round and round I go and shout,
> I am a funny roundabout.

After this, each child in turn climbs to the top of the lookout post which everyone made earlier, and he tells the others what he can see in the playground. He might say, 'A mother is comforting her child', or 'Two children are going down the slide on their tummies'. To give the child a little help, you can use a picture of a playground situation.

Aims: stimulating balance, developing appropriate body tension, body awareness, verbal memory, articulation, linking talking and moving, developing imagination

---

Materials: cushions or mats for the lookout post; a picture of a playground situation might be helpful

---

120   The boisterous kitten

The children pretend to be the kitten Mia, who dashes around the room. The adult describes what the cat is doing and the children carry out the actions:

- ◆ Mia tries to catch her own tail and, while doing this, keeps spinning around in circles. Again and again Mia tries to catch her tail.
- ◆ Mia rushes under the table.
- ◆ Mia zooms around between the long benches.
- ◆ Mia balances carefully as she walks along the long bench.
- ◆ Mia jumps off the long bench.
- ◆ Mia jumps over a box.
- ◆ Mia jumps over a bench.
- ◆ Mia jumps through a hoop.
- ◆ Mia runs around the hoop.

Mia spots a mouse. She waits in front of the box and grabs the mouse (you could use tennis balls or marbles which have been spread around the room, to represent mice – then each child tries to catch one). Later, the children take turns to describe what Mia was up to.

Aims: vestibular stimulation, developing gross motor skills, auditory attention, following verbal directions, consolidating prepositions, developing imagination

Materials: hoops; furniture such as a box, bench, table, marbles or tennis balls

121) The witches' vegetable garden

Each child draws a witch on a piece of cardboard (5cm x 10cm approx). A rubber band is attached to the back of each piece of card, so that the children can fasten their witches to a finger. Now the game can start.

A group of witches meets annually to plant two gardens. The witches turn the activity into a competition and divide into two teams.

Everyone discusses which vegetables they want to grow. Each vegetable is assigned a number on a dice (for example, 1 for beans, 2 for cucumbers, 3 for carrots, 4 for onions, 5 for tomatoes, 6 for cauliflower). You can use a worksheet illustrating the different vegetables; pictures could also be cut out of magazines and drawn, or you could use plastic vegetables as examples.

A witch must get the magic spell right for the garden gate to open. She can then slide down a slide (or something similar, like a long bench) into the garden. The magic spell to open the gate could be:

'1, 2, 3, 4, 5, make this gateway come alive!' or
'1, 2, 3, 4, magic, open up this door!' or
'1, 2, 3, in the garden let me be!'

Shorten the spell according to the ability of the children.

Once the witch has arrived in the garden, she is allowed to throw the dice. She calls out to the other witches to let them know what she is planting. Which group will be the first to plant their garden with all six vegetable types?

Aims: developing finger motor skills, articulation, stimulating a sense of balance, consolidating dice numbers and numbers 1–6

Materials: cardboard, elastic bands, pens, dice, safety scissors, pictures of vegetables, possibly a long bench or another inclined plane to serve as a slide

(122) What my hands can do

Stand in a circle around a large blanket, which has been spread out on the floor. Each child holds on to the blanket. The first child sits down in the middle of the blanket and is spun around five times by the other children: the children count the rounds. Then the blanket stops moving and the child who is sitting down demonstrates an action with their hands and says, for example:

'My hands can clap'. The children who are watching sit down and say: 'Our hands can do that, too – look, we are clapping – and beating our tummies'.

The next child sits down on the blanket, is spun for five rounds and demonstrates another action (for example, knocking, waving, rubbing, kneading, writing, grabbing, cutting, stroking, massaging, pinching, miming a noun such as a roof or a key) and verbalises the action. Again, the other children have to copy the action.

Aims: expanding vocabulary, stimulating sense of balance, developing body awareness, developing imagination, memory

Materials: blanket

(123) What my feet can do

The children stand in front of a long bench. The first child climbs on the bench, demonstrates an action and verbalises it, for example, 'My feet can stamp'. The other children now take turns to stand on the bench and copy the action while saying: 'I can stamp – and then I jump across the stream'. At the end, they jump off the bench across a marked out space (representing a stream).

Other possibilities for the actions include: balancing, walking, kicking, jumping, tripping over, marching, strutting, playing football, limping, jumping on one leg or both legs, waddling, dipping the toes in the water to the right or left, and so on.

Aims: expanding vocabulary, developing balance, imagination

Materials: long bench

(124) Tin or bin?

This game involves similar sounding words and therefore requires a certain level of concentration. Put out a tin and a bin. The adult sits between the tin and the bin and asks, for example,

'Sandra, where would you find baked beans?'
The child might answer, 'In a tin'.

The adult pretends to open a tin of beans.

If the adult asks 'Where do you put rubbish?'
The child answers, 'In the tin', because he is not yet differentiating between the sounds T and B, the adult pretends to put rubbish in the tin and the child will then try to correct his articulation.

You could use these picture cards depicting the answers: one card for 'tin' and some for baked beans, tomatoes, custard, spaghetti hoops, and so on; one card for 'bin' and some for general rubbish, such as empty cans, sweet wrappers, empty crisps packet, and so on. The child can check for himself that he has given the correct answer. The cards could be lined up at the end of a bridge (made from board, rope, long bench, chalk line or ribbon), so that the children have to balance across the bridge before being able to check if they are correct.

Aims: developing auditory differentiation between similar sounding words, differentiating between T and B, developing articulation, balance

Materials: empty tin (make sure there are no sharp edges on the tin), bin, possibly picture cards, ribbon (board, rope, long bench or chalk)

125   Washing laundry

One child pretends to be an item of clothing and lies inside a barrel or a large box representing a washing machine. The other children roll him backwards and forwards in rhythm with the following poem by Friedl Hofbauer:

Wishy washy
washing laundry
Wishy washy wumm.
Wash the top
Wash the bottom
All around.
Washing shirts, washing trousers
Washing tablecloth with roses.
Wishy washy
Washing laundry
Wishy washy wumm.
And the many trouser pockets
Turn them inside out.
Wishy washy
Washing laundry
Wishy washy
Washing laundry
Washing laundry
Wishy washy
Wumm.'
(1966, *Die Wippschaukel*, Verlag Jugend and Volk, Vienna.)

At the end of the game, the 'piece of laundry' is taken out and 'hung' on the washing line. To do this one child bends over on all fours, and another child hangs the piece of laundry (child from the washing machine) across his back. The other children pretend to be the wind which dries the laundry by making a *shshsh* sound. Then it is another child's turn to be a piece of laundry.

Aims: stimulating the vestibular system, developing memory capacity, consolidating the sound *sh*, developing proprioception

Materials: barrel, or big cardboard box

126 Box taxi

The taxi driver says a rhyme or a sentence (agreed with the adult) to invite his passenger into his vehicle. The taxi driver's rhyme could be:

Stop, box taxi – stop right there!
I will tell you when and where.
Close the door and drive along
The journey shouldn't take us long.

The children pretend to be passengers and take turns to climb into a big, strong box, which has been placed on a soft blanket. The passenger does not tell the taxi driver the destination they want to get to but, instead, directs the driver with 'left, right, straight on, back' and so on.

Materials: big cardboard box

(127) Quick journey

The children have a selection of identical picture pairs. Half of each pair is spread around the room, while the other half is put in a pile. Each child takes a card from the pile, names the picture and is pulled along on a skateboard (or a woollen blanket) to the matching card. The child can adopt different positions; he could lie on his tummy on the skateboard, with arms to the front and legs stretched out, and hold on to a knot on the rope that the adult is using to pull the board then he could be pulled along to the second card on his back, sitting cross-legged, sitting on his heels, kneeling or half-kneeling.

Materials: Skateboard (and rope) or woollen blanket, matching picture pairs

(128) A journey to the land of milk and honey

The children travel on a boat (for example, a hammock) to the land of milk and honey. During the journey they dream of all the delicious things that they are going to eat and drink there and tell one another about them. The children can also imagine some of the amazing things that they are going to see when they arrive. Once there, use mime to act out the feast and other adventures.

In the evening, it is time to travel back home. On their way home the children meet an old man and tell him about all the wonderful things they experienced in the land of milk and honey. To finish off, the children could make a boat by folding paper, or build a raft with a sail, using wood and bark. They could even put a fir cone man on the raft.

Materials: hammock (or similar); paper, wood, bar, fir cone (optional)

129 Aiming for the goal

The children take turns to sit on a swing. They try to hit a barrel with a small ball while swinging backwards and forwards. They are allowed several attempts at this. Once they get the ball in the barrel, they jump off the swing and collect a picture card. Depending on language skills they could say a word relevant to the picture, a sentence, or even make up a short story. Then it is time for the next throw.

Materials: swing, ball, barrel, picture cards

130 Look carefully!

This is a pairs game. The adult has identical picture pairs with objects representing target sounds. One set of pictures is lined up on the floor to the left and right of either a rope ladder or swing, and the adult holds on to the other pictures. Each child takes it in turn to sit on the swing or rope ladder. The adult shows the child a picture, the child tells the adult what he can see and points to the matching picture on the floor. The game becomes even more fun if you have a torch available for the child to shine onto the relevant picture.

Materials: picture pairs, swing or rope ladder, torch (optional)

(131) Land in the right place

Thick mats are spread out to make islands all around a trampoline. On these islands there are different objects or picture cards. The adult gives an instruction or shows each child a picture from their pile. The child repeats the instruction or names the picture and jumps around in a circle on the trampoline until he has discovered the relevant object or picture on one of the mats and is allowed to land there. On the mats there could, for example, be items of different shape, colour or surface characteristics, and we could ask: 'Land near a red [round, big, soft, etc] thing!'

Variation

To make the game more difficult you could work with compound nouns. The adult holds the picture cards with the first half of the compound words, and the pictures representing the second half are distributed across the mats (for example, snow – *man*, pea – *nut*). The child is given the first half of the word and has to look for a meaningful completion (to make things easier you can tell them what to look for).

Materials: thick mats, trampoline, objects (different shapes or colours), picture cards

132 Bewitched nuts

All the farm animals have been turned into nuts by a wicked witch. Now all the nuts are lying around in the woods. Of course, the farmer and his wife really want to get their animals back, before the squirrels eat up all the nuts. The children help them.

Cards depicting the different animals are spread out on the floor and a nut is placed on each picture, covering the animal. It is absolutely fine for there to be more nuts than animals – in fact, it will make it more exciting!

A magician or a good fairy tells them about a magic spell to use:

'Sim-sala-bim-am-but – away with the nut!'
'Shri-shro-shrue – who are you?'
'Kribbel -krabbel- kru – who are you?' and
'One, two, three, cut – away with the nut!'

Then the children try to move the nuts using a stick. If there is no animal under one nut, they try their luck with another or, depending on what rules have been agreed, it is the next person's turn. However, if there is an animal under the nut, the animal can be returned to the farm which is located some distance away from the woods. The animals are transported on a skateboard (representing a tractor).

Materials: picture cards of animals, nuts (or something representing nuts), skateboard

133 The animal homes are empty

A magician has turned all the animals into leaves, so all their homes (cages, stables, kennels, etc) are empty. Picture cards showing the animals are spread out in the 'forest'. On top of each card there is a leaf. However, under some of the leaves there is nothing.

Luckily, a good witch or a kind fairy appears and tells the children the magic spell to counteract the magician's spell. For example, 'Ki-ko-kee-keaf – is there someone under this leaf?' The children say the magic spell and take it in turns to take away the leaf. If there is an animal under the leaf, the child carries it out of the forest and is allowed to drive it back to their home on the skateboard or a similar piece of equipment (which could represent any type of vehicle).

The different types of animal homes could include a stable, a cage, a mousehole, a kennel, a cat basket, an aquarium, a nest, a tree trunk, a lake, a stream, etc. They could be represented through picture cards and should be arranged around the outside of the room. The children have to aim for the right home.

Materials: picture cards, leaves, skateboard (if available)

(134) Triangle, turn around!

Picture cards with objects incorporating the target sound are cut along the diagonal into two triangles. The triangles are distributed face-down, at opposite sides of the room. The children take it in turns to crawl into a barrel and are rolled backwards and forwards between the two sides. At each side the child picks up a triangle. A simple saying could be used to support practising the target sound. For example: 'Triangle, turn around!', to practise R in different word positions. Other possibilities include:

'Simsalabimbambound – triangle, turn around!'
'Shim-sham-shee-shound – triangle, turn around!'
'Hocus-pocus wirrlebound – triangle, turn around!',
and so on.

If the child manages to get two pieces that belong together, he is allowed to put the picture together and keep it. Whoever has got the most pictures in the end wins the game.

If no barrel is available, the children can simply stretch out on the ground and roll from one side of the room to the other.

Materials: picture cards, barrel (if available)

We are going on holiday

Cards depicting the items the children need to go on holiday are spread out across the room. The pictures could be cut out from a catalogue or drawn onto cardboard. Everything has simply been dropped around the 'house' and now needs to be gathered together. The picture cards are arranged in as complicated a way as possible, so the children have to climb, jump, swing, crawl and stretch – or even find aids to get to the cards. The picture cards could be attached to furniture or other objects with clothes pegs. When a child finds a card, he says: 'I have found ... I am going to pack ... in my suitcase'.

At the end, just before they leave, the children could repeat the names of all the things they have packed in the suitcase, or ask each other, 'Have you packed ...?' Alternatively, one or two of the children could unpack things in reverse order, as accurately as possible.

> **Materials:** catalogues, cardboard, picture cards, furniture, clothes pegs (optional)

(136) Hold on tight!

Beneath a hammock (or swing) there are lots of items starting with the target sound, as well as some that do not. Each child lies on his tummy across the hammock or swing and is pushed gently. He now has to collect and name all the things that begin with the target sound.

> **Materials:** hammock or swing

137 We are going shopping

Everyone puts up pictures (you could use brochures) of different shops (supermarket, furniture shop, DIY store, etc) on the walls. In addition to these there are picture cards with one item from each of the shops. (The children can cut these pictures out of a catalogue.) Each child draws a picture card and has to buy this item in the appropriate shop. To make his purchase, he lies on his tummy or kneels on a skateboard (which could represent a vehicle of his choice) and says, 'I am going to the toyshop to buy a teddy'. At the shop (in front of the picture) the shopping transaction could be acted out in role-play.

If no skateboard is available, the child can either sit down in a box which is placed on a blanket, or just on a blanket. He can then be pulled along to the shop (see also Game 126, *Box taxi*, page 177).

Materials: pictures of different shops, shopping catalogues or brochures, skateboard (alternatively, a box and/or blanket)

(138) Picture story

Each child jumps in turn on a trampoline. Thick gym mats are spread out around the trampoline. On each mat there is a picture from a picture story. The adult tells the story and, meanwhile, the child jumps around in a circle on the trampoline until he has found the corresponding picture on one of the mats.

> **Materials:** trampoline, thick gym mats, pictures from a story

(139) Rolled up in a blanket

Each child has a turn at being rolled up in a blanket. Ask him to lie down and stretch out with his head sticking out over the edge. The adult then rolls up the child and unrolls him by quickly pulling one end of the blanket. Every time the child is unrolled, he says a sentence or takes a picture card of an animal and makes a sentence about it and is rolled up again. In this way, syllables can be practised in the context of silly sentences, such as:

'Sue, sue, sue the cockerel says cock-a-doodle-doo!' or
'Soar, soar, soar, the donkey says "eeyore"!' or
'Me, me, me, I am not a little flea!' and
'Meg, meg, meg, the hen lays an egg'.

> **Materials:** blanket, picture cards of animals

140 What floats in the lake?

There are lots of different things in a box. First, the children (with eyes closed) try to guess the different objects through touch, then they sort them according to whether or not they think the objects will float. They experiment by floating them in the sink or in a bowl.

The next step involves using picture cards that depict items that float or swim in water (fish, duck, swan, wood, leaf, boat, frog, inflatable ring, ball, etc). However, there are also a few pictures of things that do not float or swim. All the picture cards lie face-down in the 'lake' and have a paper clip attached to them. The children take turns to catch the pictures using a 'fishing rod' (a stick with a bit of a string and a magnet attached to the end of the string). However, they are only allowed to fish from the boat (possibly represented by a hammock or swing).

While fishing, say a sentence containing a target sound, for example: 'There is a … swimming/floating in the water' (lake, pond, river, sea, puddle); or 'I have caught a …'. Who has caught the most things that can swim/float and has got the most of the non-floating items?

Materials: box, objects, bowl (or sink), picture cards, paper clip, rod (stick with string and magnet), hammock or swing (optional)

Animal magic

Build a house using gym mats. In the house lives a friendly magician. He can turn everyone into different animals, according to their wishes. However, the children must first swing on a rope across the magic lake to the magician's castle and knock on the door with their feet. Then the magician comes out and turns the child into an animal. The magic spell could be:

'Hocus-pocus – wimmel-wammel-wound,
As horses you now walk around!'
Variations on the second part could be
'As elephants you now stamp around!' or
'As bees you now hum around!', and so on.

The spell lasts until the magician stamps his foot on the floor. Then the child who has been enchanted has to swing across the lake again and is turned into a different animal. The game becomes even funnier if you play suitable music for the different animals.

Materials: gym mats, rope swing

(142) Will the tunnel open? (1)

Everyone builds a tunnel with a gate in front of it. Using a skateboard, the children take it in turns to follow a certain route to the gate. In front of the gate, each child has to say a magic spell in order for the gate to open – then he is allowed, without using his hands, to nibble a small salt pretzel from a piece of string. Finally, the child can be off on his way again. The magic spell could be, 'Ree-ra-rate, open the gate!'

Materials: tunnel, gate, skateboard, pretzel on a string

(143) Journey to Africa

Everyone is travelling to Africa on a ship (represented by a hammock), because they want to see the different animals there. On board the ship they order all kinds of different food and drinks and make plans about Africa. Each child climbs up an observation tower (for example, a rope ladder). He then looks around with a home-made telescope to see whether he can spot something interesting and calls down to let everyone else know.

Once the ship arrives in Africa, the children go for a walk on a bridge from which they are going to watch crocodiles. Of course, they have to summon up a lot of courage to do this:

'I have courage, brave and true, there is nothing I can't do!' or

'I am strong and I am great, I can watch crocodiles till late!' or

'Hocus-pocus magic trick, give me lots of power – quick!'

The big crocodiles are not visible, but the baby crocodiles (represented by clothes pegs) are lying on the beach. Everybody takes a baby crocodile and pretends to make the clothes peg speak by opening and closing it using thumb and index finger. For example, the crocodiles could be saying, 'I am a crocodile and I love eating. My favourite food is …' Perhaps you could have some food available (for example, crackers) that could be pegged up above the baby crocodiles.

Everyone continues across mountains and through valleys (a few chairs are lined up one behind the other and the children have to go under and over the chairs in turn) until they get to the elephants. You could sing an elephant song, for example, *Nelly the elephant*, and stamp along to it. To finish off, the children pretend to be elephants and carry logs to a particular destination by holding Twiglets between their lips or between their upper lip and their nose.

Materials: hammock, ropeladder, home-made telescope, clothes pegs, crackers (or similar), chairs, Twiglets

Enchanted stones

Depending on the target sound or the interests of the child, different things are selected for the magician to put a spell on and turn into stones. They could be animals, household objects, groceries, fancy dress costumes, tools, toys, fruit, vegetables, seeds or plants, garden tools, Christmas tree decorations, ingredients for a cookie recipe, swimming things, things you would put in a rucksack to go on a hike, winter sports equipment or clothes.

Whatever the magician has turned into stones is needed urgently (stones have either been made from paper by the children or they have collected real stones) so everyone asks the witch for help. The witch checks in her magic spells book and finds a spell to change things back into their original state. The magic spell could be:

'Ki-ko-kone, away with the stone!'
'Kli-klo-klone, away with the stone!'
'Kri-kro-krone – away with the stone!'
'Fri-fro-frone, away with the stone!' or
'She-sho-shone, away with the stone!', and so on.

Pictures of the things that have been enchanted are lying underneath the stones. For every stone the children find they say the magic spell and then take the stone away to see what is underneath it. If the magic spell is not articulated correctly, it is not possible to take the stone away! The enchanted stones are put between bricks (representing little islands), on which the child who is lifting the stones has to balance.

Variation

The magician could also turn the different things into eggs, which he could, for example, put into birds' nests. Accordingly, the magic spell could be, 'See-so-segg, away with the egg!' and so on. The birds' nests should be attached somewhere higher up, so that the children have to climb or swing themselves there on a rope.

Materials: stones (or ones hand-made out of paper), toy bricks, pictures of a selected topic. For the variation: hand-made eggs and birds nests

(145) Jump over the string

Tie a piece of thin rope or string between two chairs. Place different objects around it or alternatively, use picture cards which have been cut out of a catalogue. Categories could be fruit, vegetables, tools, wooden toys, plastic toys, cutlery, crockery, clothes, musical instruments, writing utensils, fastenings, containers, electrical appliances and furniture, etc.

The children are given the task of collecting things that belong to a particular category (for example, all the tools). However, in order to collect something, they have to jump over the string. If the string is tied at an angle to the floor, every child can find a height that matches their level of ability.

> **Materials:** thin rope or string, two chairs, picture cards

(**146**) Enchanted fish

Depending on the target sound or the interests of the individual children, different objects (picture cards) are selected, which the magician then turns into fish. To do this, the objects or picture cards are spread out in the lake (which could be an area marked out on the floor) and a cardboard fish with a paper clip attached to it is placed onto each item. Each child is given a fishing rod (a stick with a piece of a string and a magnet on the end of it) and now has to try to catch the fish. However, he is only allowed to move along the bank (which could be a narrow band of floor space) or on islands in the water (could be represented by building blocks); he is not allowed to step in the water. While the child is fishing, he says, for example,

'Hocus-pocus, zish, away with the fish!'

When he manages to catch a fish, he can have a look to see what is underneath it, take the item, name it and put the picture onto a lotto board or a puzzle.

> **Materials:** picture cards, paper clips, stick, magnet, string (for fishing rod), lotto board

(147) Caution! Electric fence!

Tie a string between two chairs and place a table behind it. Set out a selection of small objects on the table. The distance between the children and the string depends on the average height of the children – they should just be able to reach the objects on the table by bending forward without touching the string. Now pretend that the string is an electric fence, which must be touched under no circumstances. Only by carefully bending forward can everyone recover the things that the robber has stolen from the princess. People take turns telling each other what they are going to recover, and then carefully reach out to retrieve the item.

> **Materials:** string, two chairs, table, a selection of objects

(148) We are going to the circus

For this game you need a pair of stilts. Stilts can either be bought or, together with the children, you can make a good pair of stilts from tin cans by drilling two holes facing each other in the top of the cans, threading through some thick string and tying it together for each can. To use the stilts, the children stand on the cans and hold the string tight with their hands. Using the string, the cans are pulled up to lift the feet, so the child can walk (you need to adjust the length of the strings according to the height of the child).

Using the stilts, the children try to get to the circus, which is stopping in town today. In the circus there is a clown (adult, finger or hand puppet or a larger rag doll), who shows them some funny tricks. The clown also shows them pictures of the other circus artists. Anyone can ask questions, and the clown tries to answer everything he is asked. However, sometimes he is a bit silly and tells the children things that don't happen in the real world.

Materials: stilts (bought or made), clown puppet, pictures of circus performers

(149) Treasure hunt

Treasure is hidden for the children to find. However, they have to use stilts (see Game 148, *We are going to the circus*, page 199) to reach it. Each child is given a piece of paper, on which the first stop of the treasure hunt is marked. At that stop the child will find another piece of paper with further instructions. The treasure hunt should have about five stops before the treasure is discovered.

Materials: stilts, paper, treasure

150 Snail

A snail is drawn on the floor and divided into as many spaces as a chosen rhyme has syllables. The children jump along the spaces without touching the lines and back again. Whoever manages to jump the whole snail without touching the lines is allowed to put something in one of the spaces. This space then has to be jumped over in the next round.

Once everyone has practised the jumping, they can start saying the rhyme. For those spaces that have to be jumped over, they only say the corresponding word or syllable very quietly. If jumping over spaces is too difficult for some children, they could have some other 'reward' for successfully completing the course and reciting the rhyme.

Materials: chalk

(151) Magic stones

A road is marked out on the floor using string or chalk lines. On this road are a lot of stones (glass pebbles, or beanbags). These stones are magic stones which must not be touched. The children have to walk on stilts (see Game 148, *We are going to the circus*, page 199) across the stones. At the end of the road, each child has to tell us what colour the stones are. He is also allowed to reach into a magic trunk, guess what he has got in his hand, and then take the object out. If the child touched a magic stone on his way, the trunk won't open and the child has to try the walk again.

Materials: chalk or string, stones (glass pebbles or beanbags), stilts, magic trunk, assorted small objects

---

152 Crossing the stream

A stream is marked out on the floor using string or chalk lines. This stream needs to be crossed with the help of three 'stones' (cardboard discs, beer mats or real, flat stones). The children stand on two stones and are allowed to move the third stone using their hand. Where the stream originates there is a dragon's lair. The dragon (for example, a sock hand puppet or a peg dinosaur as in Game 101, *Dinosaur game*, page 144) has captured someone and is keeping them prisoner. The children might even need to say a special sentence to summon up enough courage. The dragon will only let the person or animal go free if a child can solve three riddles or problems. The riddles or problems could be:

◆ How many sunflower seeds (or raisins) have I put on your tongue?
◆ Smelly containers: can you find two containers with the same smell?
◆ Where has the alarm clock been hidden? (Directional listening!)

If cardboard tiles are used as stones, each tile could have a different surface to provide the child with different touch sensations.

Materials: string or chalk, 3 stones (discs or beer mats), 'dragon' puppet, props for problem-solving

---

(153) Shops across the bridge

The children are given shopping lists which have pictures
(either drawn or glued on) of things they have to buy.
The shops (use pictures, as in Game 137, *We are going
shopping*, page 187) are on the other side of the 'stream'.
This means that each child has to cross a bridge. The
bridge could be a board that has been placed across two
chairs, or a long bench. First the child needs to decide
what he needs to buy and where, and then he needs to
visit the corresponding shops.

> **Materials:** illustrated shopping list, 'shop' pictures,
> two chairs and board or long bench

Part 3: Listening Games

Many children have auditory perception difficulties due to an overload of sensory stimulation from their environment. The following games aim to train children's ability to react to auditory signals and focus listening attention on auditory stimuli. Perceiving and differentiating noises and sounds is practised through a variety of activities which ultimately aim to improve articulation and, to some extent, sentence formulation.

Many of these auditory differentiation games require words containing specific sounds or sound sequences. If you are unable to think of enough words immediately, simply take a dictionary or encyclopaedia and look up a given initial letter.

As with all the other games, the activities in this section aim to stimulate as many senses as possible in order to provide essential 'basic training' for the brain.

The games listed as auditory discrimination exercises also facilitate the development of general listening skills (see Part 6, Games for working on specific speech sound problems).

(154) Looking for noises together

The adult calls two children by their names without looking at them. Those two children have to get together as a pair and close their eyes, while something that makes a noise (for example, a small alarm clock or radio) is hidden in their clothing. They then have to feel each other with the palms of their hands to find the source of the noise. Then it is another pair's turn.

Aims: consolidating children's names, developing physical contact, tactile perception, tolerating touch, developing auditory perception, mutual leading and following, being still and waiting patiently for your turn

> **Materials:** something that makes a noise (for example, a small alarm clock or radio)

(155) Clapping names

The children take it in turns to clap out the syllables of each other's name and jump to the rhythm of the syllables.

For the second round, two children at a time face each other and clap out the rhythm of the syllables of their names on the palms of each other's hands.

Aims: consolidating children's names, developing auditory perception, improving sense of rhythm, physical contact

Materials: none

(156) Name echo

The children sit in a circle and one child starts the game by clearly and deliberately saying the syllables of their name: 'I – mo – gen'. All the other children pretend to be echoes and clap out the syllables without speaking.

Following this activity, each child has a turn to clap, use their fingers to snap, or use their feet to stamp out a rhythm. The other children have to copy the rhythm and find a matching name.

Aims: consolidating children's names, developing auditory perception, improving sense of rhythm

Materials: none

Alphabet names

The aim is for children to try to organise themselves according to the initial letters of their names. To do this you need letter tiles or magnetic letters.

The children move around the room like a train, with their hands on the shoulders of the person in front of them and slowly walk past the letter tiles. The adult starts by showing the children a letter asking: 'Which name begins with A?' (then B, C, and so on). Each name is said in turn and everyone decides whether the name begins with that letter or not. If the name begins with the announced letter, the child gets off the train and stands with his letter tile. The remaining children continue as a train.

Once all children have got off at a letter tile, they try to represent the letter using their body. Some of the letters will have more than one child, making letter representation particularly funny.

Aims: developing auditory sound discrimination, initial sound identification, tactile sensation, imagination

Materials: letter tiles or magnetic letters

(158) Interview with a puppet

For younger children, a puppet comes to visit and tells them about his holidays, then asks each child in turn what they got up to in their own holidays. He clowns around and misunderstands some of the things they say.

For older children, a reporter with a microphone could replace the puppet and interview the children. He, too, keeps misunderstanding things, perhaps because there is a storm blowing or because the interview is carried out next to a noisy building site, making it difficult to hear.

Here are some examples of the dialogue which could ensue:

Child: 'I went on a boat.' – '*Puppet*: 'What do you mean, you went on a coat?'
Child: 'I walked up a mountain.' – *Puppet*: 'What about a fountain?'
Child: 'I did some diving in the sea.' – *Puppet*: 'Where were you driving?'

The child will want to correct the puppet and will subsequently try particularly hard to speak clearly, so the puppet can understand.

Aims: having fun talking, developing auditory perception

Materials: puppet, reporter, 'microphone' (eg, made from an empty toilet roll or tennis ball)

159 Which word begins with the same sound as 'ball'?

Think about the sound B and look at how it is produced (air popping out from closed lips). Everyone practises saying several B-B-B sounds in sequence and compares these with a bouncing ball (the ball, too, begins with B).

The adult says different words for the children. If a word starts with B, each child bounces their ball on the floor. On command (perhaps to a drum beat) each child collects their own ball. This means that they have to carefully keep an eye on, and follow, their ball. They then wait for the next B-word. The game can also be played without the command, and the children simply wait until the balls have come to a stop.

Variation
Vary the game with questions such as, 'Which word begins with the same sound as 'branch'?' – the children have to stretch up their arms and sway their upper bodies back and forth, pretending to be a tree or a branch swaying in the wind. At a visual signal, the wind stops, and the children wait for the next B-word.

Aims: developing auditory attention and discrimination, sound identification, visual perception, concentration, ability to react, body control

Materials: balls, possibly a drum

Puppet mess

The puppet shows the children a picture of a table which has got various portable items on it and a picture of a shop selling electrical appliances (things that have a cable). There is also a table and an area marked as a 'cable' shop (which the children could build themselves). The puppet has made a bit of a mess. The children have to help him to put things in the right place.

The puppet takes an object or a picture card and asks the children: 'Where does the plate belong? Table or cable?' One child answers: 'Table', and the puppet puts the plate on the table. 'Where does the washing machine belong? Table or cable?' The child might say 'table', because he is not yet differentiating between the sounds T and C, so the puppet will try to put the washing machine on the table. The child is likely to protest and try and correct himself.

Aims: developing visual perception, visual memory, auditory discrimination of similar sounds (C, T), improving articulation

Materials: puppet, pictures of a table and an appliances shop/brochure, pictures or objects

(161) Rain – lane

It is common for children to mix up the sounds R and L: specifically, R is often replaced by L. The words 'rain' and 'lane' sound very similar. In this game, the children have to concentrate in order to differentiate the words and also to try to articulate them correctly. If an L is said instead of an R, this can lead to funny sentences.

The adult provides the child with an unfinished sentence, into which the child has to insert the correct word. The child whose turn it is climbs up on a platform (perhaps a table or chair) and calls out the matching word. The other children mime the suggested word. If the word is 'rain', they move their arms up and down to represent the rain. If the word is 'lane', they line up behind each other and 'drive' once around the room.

You might provide the children with sentences such as these:

Yesterday there was a lot of …
The tractor drove down the …
The boy got soaked by the …
The little girl lived down the …
Flowers need lots of …
Drive carefully down that narrow …
I had to stay inside because there was so much …
Jack walked slowly along the …

Aims: developing auditory perception, auditory discrimination of similar sounds R and L, gross motor skills, coordination, body awareness, being gentle, improving articulation

Materials: none

162 Where is the conker going to roll?

The children close their eyes. A conker is rolled through the room. The children have to follow the movement of the conker by moving their arms to point to the conker. Once the conker has stopped they can open their eyes and check whether they are pointing in the right direction.

Variations
The child closes his eyes. A conker is rolled. Moving his arm, the child has to indicate the direction the conker is rolling. Once it has stopped, the child has to open his eyes, check where the conker is, and then crawl to the conker with his eyes closed.

Older children could estimate how many steps they would need to get to the conker and then walk towards it with their eyes closed.

Aims: developing auditory perception, listening carefully, orientating around a room, developing body awareness

Materials: conker

163 Which word begins with the same sound as 'flag'?

Each child makes himself a flag. While the music is playing, the children move in a specific way between hoops or pieces of newspaper on the floor. When the music stops, each child has to stand in a hoop or on a piece of newspaper. The adult calls out different words. If a word starts with F (or FL), each child lifts his flag and swings it through the air in a figure of eight; if the word does not begin with F (or FL), the flags stay down. In this way, you can practise discriminating between similar sounds, such as S and F or simply identify F as an initial sound.

Aims: developing auditory perception and discrimination, reaction, crossing the midline

Materials: paper for flags, sticks or plastic straws for flagpoles, music, newspaper or hoops

Foil or soil?

Pieces of newspaper have been spread out on the floor – one piece fewer than there are children. While the music is playing, the children walk around between the pieces of newspaper with their flags (see Game 163, *Which word begins with the same sound as 'flag'?*, page 216). When the music stops, each child has to stand on a piece of newspaper. Because there is one piece less than there are children, one child will be left without a newspaper to stand on. This child is given a riddle. The adult asks the child: 'What do you put sandwiches [or rolls, ham, flowers, plants, seeds, etc] in? – Foil or soil?'

Using toy food or laminated picture cards, you could also try to put the child's answers into practice. So, if the child says, 'We put sandwiches in soil', and you attempt to bury a sandwich in soil, the child will try to correct his articulation to get the intended result.

Aims: developing auditory perception, reaction, room orientation, discriminating between similar sounding speech sounds S and F, improving articulation

Materials: home-made flags, newspaper, music, possibly foil, soil, toy food and plastic flowers/plants or picture cards depicting food and plants, flowers, seeds

(165) Does the word start with the same sound as 'dragon'?

Children often mix up, or are unable to differentiate between, the consonant clusters *dr* and *gr*. The following game helps with this. Together with the children, fold a kite and draw a dragon on it. For the dragon's tail, small pieces of plastic straws could be threaded on to a piece of string, using a needle. A string for flying the dragon is attached to each kite.

Say words beginning with DR and GR. If the word starts with DR, for 'dragon', the children are allowed to fly their kites running as fast as they can and pulling the dragon kites along behind them. At a visual signal, all children sit down again and wait for the next word.

Aims: developing finger motor skills, auditory attention and sound discrimination, gross motor skills, speed, visual perception

Materials: paper, glue, pens, string, plastic straws, safety scissors, thread, needle

166 Does the word start with the same sound as 'snow'?

If it has snowed, this game can be played outside. The adult says different words. Some begin with SN, some don't. If a word begins with SN, the children are allowed to throw a snowball at a given target. If a word does not begin with SN, the children are only allowed to prepare snowballs. If you play this game indoors, the children could make, and shoot, paper balls.

Aims: developing auditory attention and discrimination, hand-eye control, finger motor skills

> **Materials:** outdoors – none, indoors – newspaper or tissue paper

Snowball box match

This game requires two players or two teams of players. Two boxes are placed next to each other in the snow. In front of the boxes there is a line to shoot from and, approximately 4-5m behind the boxes, there is a finish line. First of all, each child makes up a stash of snowballs. Then different words are called out. The children are allowed to fire a snowball at their box each time they hear a word beginning with SN. Which box will make it first across the finish line? If you play this game indoors, use tennis balls instead of snowballs.

Aims: developing hand motor skills, auditory discrimination, reaction, hand-eye control

Materials: snowballs (or tennis balls), boxes

(168) Still exercise with candles

All of the children sit in a circle. On hearing an auditory signal, the children close their eyes and are only allowed to open them when they hear exactly the same signal again. While the children have got their eyes closed, a bowl of water is placed in the middle of the circle. Next to the bowl is a burning candle. In addition, there is a selection of tea lights (floating candles). Then the signal is given for the second time and the children are allowed to look. The adult tells the children a story.

The children all think of wishes they would like to make. (These wishes should not be of a materialistic nature.) If a child would like to make a wish, he takes a tea light and gives it to the adult, who lights it using the burning candle and places it on the water. The child then says his wish out loud. Everybody closes their eyes, quietly hopes that the wish will come true and waits for the next signal to open their eyes. Again, a child is allowed to make a wish and place a tea light onto the water. At the end, everybody joins hands and wishes for everyone's wishes to come true. Afterwards, children are allowed to take turns in blowing out one tea light – carefully without blowing out any of the other flames.

Aims: developing auditory perception, sensitising sense of perception, developing attention control, providing for the need to feel safe, calming down, being open with other people, listening to others, developing gentleness, self-expression, talking about feelings

Materials: bowl, water, candle, tea lights (floating candles), auditory signal

(169) Tea or key?

The children have to listen carefully during this game, which uses the similar sounding words 'tea' and 'key'. It requires jigsaw puzzles of a teapot or a cup of tea and a key, which you could make yourself with the children's help. The number they throw on a dice decides whether they receive a jigsaw piece for 'tea' or a jigsaw piece for 'key': If a child throws a 1, 2 or 3, they receive a piece of the 'tea' puzzle. If they throw a 4, 5 or 6, they receive a piece of the 'key' puzzle. For younger children, pictures of 'tea' and 'key' could be drawn onto the sides of a blank dice – then the child will throw, for example, a teacup or a key picture. If a child throws a number for a puzzle piece but has already completed the respective jigsaw, he has been unlucky and receives nothing.

The adult plays the shopkeeper. If a child throws a 3, he has to go to the shopkeeper and request, 'A piece of 'tea', please'. If the child has difficulties differentiating between T and K, this game will encourage him to improve his articulation. The player who finishes first is the winner. The game can also be played in two groups; which group will complete their puzzles first?

Aims: developing hand-eye coordination (when drawing and cutting), developing auditory discrimination between the similar sounding speech sounds T and K, articulation, visual perception, understanding of quantity

Materials: cardboard and pens to make the jigsaw puzzles, safety scissors, dice

170 Which word begins with the same sound as 'ten'?

Each child writes a large number 10 on their piece of paper and divides it into 10 parts. The adult says lots of different words. Every time a word begins with T for 'ten', the children are allowed to colour in one part of their number. If the word does not begin with T, the children have to wait. The adult should vary between words that have very different initial sounds to T and words that begin with T or K, in order to practise discrimination of similar initial sounds.

Aims: developing auditory attention, sound identification, auditory discrimination, concentration, hand-eye coordination, reaction

Materials: paper, pens

The four seasons game

The children spread out picture cards of the four seasons (see Game 18, *The four seasons*, page 43) on the floor around the room. While the music is playing, the children have to walk around the picture cards without touching them. When the music stops, the adult or a designated child calls out a season, and the children quickly have to stand with their legs straddled across a matching picture. Everyone checks each other to make sure they have got the correct picture.

Aims: developing auditory attention, assigning appropriate pictures to seasons, developing reaction, room orientation

Materials: seasonal pictures, music

 Balloon trampoline

The children hold a large cloth around the edges. One or more balloons are placed on the cloth. Then a story about a balloon is told and each time the children hear the word 'balloon', the balloon is thrown up into the air by lifting the cloth and then caught again.

Aims: developing auditory perception and differentiation, reaction, agility

Materials: balloon, large cloth (eg tablecloth, sheet)

(173) Does the word start with the magic sound 'Z'?

Each child is given a piece of newspaper and stands on it. Different words are spoken. If a word begins with Z, each child steps off their piece of newspaper, holds it in front of their chest or tummy and tries to walk so quickly that his piece of newspaper does not fall down, so that the child is holding it without using their hands.

At an agreed signal, each child stands on his piece of newspaper again and waits for the next word beginning with Z, then tries to do his magic trick of using a headwind to fix the piece of paper to his chest or tummy. Because the children have to walk as quickly as possible for this game, a large room is required. This game can be played particularly well outdoors, especially on a windy day.

Aims: developing auditory attention and sound discrimination, gross motor skills, speed, visual attention

---

Materials: newspapers

---

174 Nonsense sentence

The children take partners, then sit in a circle (each pair face to face) and listen carefully. To make sure they are listening attentively, ask them to stroke their ears and tickle their ear lobes. Then the adult offers different sentences, one after the other. If the content of the sentence is wrong or does not make sense, the children shout, 'Nonsense!', and clap their hands twice. If the sentence is correct, the two partners first clap their right, and then their left palms together (ie, across the midline) and shout out 'Correct!'

Try using sentences like these:

- ◆ The horse is sitting in the car.
- ◆ The pig is flying.
- ◆ The exercise book belongs to the pupil.
- ◆ The monkey uses its wings to climb.
- ◆ The duck swims.
- ◆ The sun shines at night.
- ◆ Apples are growing on the tree.
- ◆ The fish are swimming through the garden.
- ◆ The lamp is hanging under the table.
- ◆ The soup is cooking in the fridge.

Aims: developing auditory attention, reaction, physical contact, coordination

Materials: none

(175) Which word begins with the same sound as 'caterpillar'?

The adult says different words, some beginning with the K (/k/) sound (for 'caterpillar'), and others which do not. If a word begins with a 'K' sound, the children have to use their fingers and pretend there is a caterpillar crawling across their partner's hand. If possible, index finger, middle finger, ring finger and little finger should tap in sequence. If the word does not begin with a 'K' sound, the caterpillar has a rest.

Aims: developing auditory attention and discrimination, reaction, tactile sensation, finger motor skills

Materials: none

176 Mother cat

One child pretends to be the mother cat and two children pretend to be kittens. The mother cat sits with her kittens in the middle of the circle. She has her eyes closed and is sleeping. All the other children pretend to be foxes, who want to sneak up on the kittens. If the mother can hear them, she looks up, hisses *chchch* and tries to scratch the fox(es) (make sure the children only touch rather than scratch each other). The first fox touched by the mother cat becomes the new mother cat.

Aims: practising and consolidating the sound *ch*, auditory attention, gentleness, agility

Materials: none

177 Which word begins with the same sound as 'frog'?

All the children pretend to be frogs in a pond, which could be represented by a large chalk circle. The adult says different words; some begin with *fr*, and some do not. If a word begins with *fr*, the children have to jump out of the pond with a giant leap. If the word does not begin with *fr*, the frogs won't want to jump.

Aims: developing auditory perception, auditory discrimination, gross motor skills

Materials: chalk

(178) Blossom magic

This is a good game for spring. Each child scrunches up a square of brightly coloured cloth (tie-dyed material would work well) or a thin scarf until it is small enough to fit into the fist. Then the children say a magic spell, wait for an auditory signal and slowly open up their fists. Each cloth should start to come out, and slowly unfold like a blossom. The cloth looks fascinating as it unfolds and encourages focused looking.

An auditory signal (eg, a crash of a cymbal) represents the sun. When the sun comes out from behind the clouds, the blossom opens up. If the sun disappears behind the clouds (accompanied by scratching on the cymbal), the blossom folds up again – in other words, the fist again closes, scrunching up the cloth. Now do some more magic and wait for the sun. The magic spell could be, for example: 'Hocus-pocus, witch's cup – beautiful blossom open up'.

Aims: developing auditory perception, reaction, concentration, gentleness, articulation

Materials: brightly coloured cloth/thin scarf for each child, cymbal

(179) Spring picture

The children are given paper and coloured pens. The adult describes a picture for them, and the children have to draw according to the adult's description. In order to avoid problems with left and right, each child is allowed to have sticker on their right hand. Here is an example:

'On the left side, there is a house. The house has two windows and one door. On the roof, there is a chimney. There is smoke coming from the chimney. To the right of the house there are two trees. Two flowers are growing underneath the right tree. There is a washing line stretched between the two trees. On the washing line there are three socks and one pair of trousers. The sun is shining. I can see four clouds in the sky.'

Then compare your drawings. Who has forgotten anything?

Aims: developing listening attention, orientating on paper, left-right discrimination

Materials: paper, coloured pens

(**180**) Birdsongs

The children stand opposite each other in pairs, lift their arms and touch each other's palms, thus building a tunnel. Then the children make up different birdsongs, for example: *peep-peep, crar-crar, ziwitt-ziwitt, tong-tong, gru-gru, tree-tree, cocoo-cocoo, pink-pink, zwee-zwee*, and so on. Each pair sings their own birdsong.

One child leaves the room, and the remaining pairs agree on one birdsong. The child is asked to return to the room and has to recognise a specific bird pair, for example, the crows singing, *crar-crar*. Then all the other pairs copy that song. The child has to walk through the tunnel with his eyes closed, and stop when he thinks he has got to the correct pair. If he is right, that pair catch the child in their arms and briefly hold on to him.

The same game can also be played with any vowel, consonant or sound sequence.

Aims: improving articulation (especially consonant clusters), developing auditory differentiation, directional hearing, tactile sensation

Materials: none

(181) Looking for a nest

All of the children form a big circle. One child pretends to be a young bird, going into the middle of the circle and closes his eyes. He has fallen out of the nest. Another child in the circle pretends to be the bird's mother and calls with her birdsong. The young bird now has to find his mum with his eyes closed. If he finds his way back into the nest, the bird's mother becomes the young bird.

Birdsongs are a great way of practising consonant clusters such as *crar-crar, gru-gru, tree-tree, zwui-zwui, zwee-zwee*, and so on.

Aims: developing directional hearing, articulation of consonant clusters

Materials: none

(182) Finding a bird partner

In pairs, the children agree on a birdsong (see Game 180, *Birdsongs*, page 233). Then the children spread out around the room, close their eyes and on 'Go!' start walking, each singing his birdsong and trying to find his partner, who will be singing the same song.

Aims: developing auditory differentiation, directional hearing, room orientation

Materials: none

(183) Looking for eggs

Children always like to play hide-and-seek games. One child closes his eyes while the other children hide an 'egg' (hard-boiled egg, pebble, or small toy). Then the first child is allowed to look for the egg. The other children are allowed to help by shouting 'hot' (meaning he is near the hiding place) or 'cold' (he is moving away from the hiding place). Once the child has found the egg, he tells the reporter where he found the egg: 'The egg was hidden behind the cupboard'. The reporter records this on tape.

At the end, everyone tries to remember the sequence in which the eggs were hidden, as well as their hiding places. The children take it in turns to say where they discovered their egg. You can use the tape to help check both the sequence and the hiding places.

Aims: practising auditory attention, developing reaction, visual perception, prepositions, articulation, memory

Materials: 'eggs', tape recorder or another recording device

184 Which word begins with the same sound as 'singing'?

The adult says different words. Some begin with S, while some do not.

If a word begins with S, like 'singing', each child has to use his finger to draw the letter S on the back of another child while making the sound *sss*.

If the word does not begin with S, the children stroke each other's backs with flat hands. This game works best if the children all sit one behind the other in a circle.

Aims: developing auditory attention and differentiation (ie, identifying the sound S), reaction, tactile sensation, body awareness, articulation of the sound S

Materials: none

185 Which word begins with the same sound as 'puddle'?

The adult says different words. Some begin with P, some do not.

If a word begins with P, the children have to jump over a puddle (which could be a newspaper, a carpet tile, etc) with both feet. If a word does not begin with P, the children sit down next to the puddle. After each word, the children return to the start, walking on all fours.

You can either use very different sounding initial sounds, or you can contrast P with similar sounding sounds, or with sounds that the child is mixing up with P. Draw the children's attention to the lip closure required to produce the plosive P.

Aims: developing auditory attention and sound discrimination, visual perception, gross motor skills, body coordination, proprioception, reaction

Materials: newspaper or carpet tiles

186 Face or saucepan?

Children often confuse the sounds F and S. This game helps children to think about and control their articulation. On one piece of paper, draw the outline of a face, and on the other draw a saucepan. You will also need pictures of different facial parts and of different vegetables. The vegetable pictures have words beginning with S stuck to the back, while the facial parts pictures have words beginning with F stuck to the back.

Everyone works together to complete the face, as well as assemble the ingredients for a vegetable soup in the saucepan.

The adult holds the vegetable and facial parts picture cards, as well as the pieces of paper with the outlines of the face and the saucepan. During the game, she hands over the picture card and the picture of the face or saucepan which corresponds to the child's answer.

To begin playing, the adult picks a picture card and reads the word on the back. The child has to decide whether the word starts start with F for 'face', or S for 'saucepan'. If the child gives the wrong answer (because he is not differentiating well between the two sounds) he will end up with a picture card that does not match the outline on the main picture (eg, a vegetable picture card and the face outline). The child can check for himself that he is

correct by looking at the letter on the back of the picture card. The child will try hard to get his articulation right in order to complete the pictures – especially if some reward is offered for picture completion!

Aims: developing auditory perception, auditory discrimination between similar sounding words (F/S minimal pairs) and sounds, finger motor skills, vocabulary

---

Materials: paper, pens, picture cards of vegetables, facial parts, face outline and saucepan – you could draw these together with the child before playing the game

---

(187) Body noises

All of the children close their eyes. One child begins the game, making a noise with his body. The others have to guess how the child has made that noise and try to copy it. Possible noises include: stamping; clapping; clicking the fingers; clicking the tongue; slurping; exploding the lips (P-P-P); drumming on the chest with or without voice; rubbing the hands; walking on the heels, and so on.

Aims: developing auditory perception and differentiation, vocabulary, body awareness

Materials: none

(188) Noise quiz

Different unbreakable objects are put out and named. One child turns his back to the others, closes his eyes and listens. Another child drops one of the objects. The first child now has to guess the object dropped by the noise it makes when it falls on the floor, saying perhaps: 'The spoon has landed!', or 'The dice has fallen on the floor!', or 'You dropped the scissors!'

Aims: developing auditory perception and differentiation, articulation

Materials: a selection of unbreakable objects

189 Which ball has dropped?

One child closes his eyes. Different balls (tennis ball, table tennis ball, softball, gym ball, paper ball) have been placed in a box. One ball is dropped and the child has to guess which ball it was. He fetches the ball and throws it back into the box with the other balls from an agreed distance. Then it is the next child's turn.

Aims: developing auditory attention and differentiation, hand-eye coordination, vocabulary

---

Materials: a box with a selection of balls such as a tennis ball, table tennis ball, softball, gym ball, paper ball

---

(190) Does the word begin with the same sound as 'crocodile'?

Many children have difficulty discriminating between the consonant clusters /kr/ and /tr/. The following game requires them to listen extra carefully.

Baby crocodiles (use clothes pegs) have been spread around the room. The adult says different words beginning with /kr/ or /tr/. If a word begins with *kr*, each child has to take a baby crocodile and try to 'bite' another child by attaching the clothes peg to the other child's clothing. Afterwards, the clothes pegs are taken off, and the crocodiles lie in the sun again. If a word does not begin with /kr/, the crocodiles continue lying in the sun.

Aims: developing auditory attention and speech sound discrimination, reaction, finger motor skills, dexterity, speed

Materials: clothes pegs

(191) Train journey

Build a tunnel and a mountain for this train journey. All of the children link up, putting their hands on the shoulders of the person in front of them, and move around the room like a train making a *sh-sh-sh* sound. The child at the head of the column is the train driver.

One place in the room has been chosen as a platform where the train always has to stop. When the train reaches the platform, the train driver becomes a platform attendant and is given a signalling disc. The adult shows a picture card or says a word. If the child can hear a *sh* in the word, he is allowed to give the train a signal to continue its journey but if the word does not have a *sh*, the train has to wait.

Once the train is allowed to move on, the platform attendant gives back the signalling disc, jumps on the back of the train, and the child at the front becomes the train driver.

Aims: developing auditory perception and speech sound discrimination, reaction, body awareness

---

Materials: signalling disc, possibly picture cards

---

192 Fairy lake

The children get together in pairs, and each pair is given a hoop. If a word begins with S, both children jump into the lake, represented by the hoop on the floor, and make swimming movements, while standing on one leg. If a word begins with F, one child pretends to be a fairy and has to walk around inside the hoop without touching the sides, while his partner holds it at hip height. After each word, the children take turns to roll the hoop and try catching it before it falls on the floor.

If the children find it very difficult to discriminate between the two sounds, it is better for them to focus on listening out for one sound only (ie, either F or S) and carry out the matching movement.

Aims: developing auditory attention and speech sound discrimination, balance, coordination, agility and dexterity, physical contact, developing gentleness, tactile awareness

Materials: hoops

(193) Shower bath

This listening game can be played outside on a nice, hot summer's day. The adult says many different compound words. If a word contains the word 'water', the children have to run under the jet of a hosepipe or the spray of a watering can. If the compound word does not contain the word 'water', the children have to run away as quickly as possible so that they don't get sprayed. Of course, the children could also have a turn selecting words.

Variation
If any child can think of a sentence containing the word 'water', he is allowed to run under the spray. You could also move the hosepipe or watering can rhythmically up and down so that the child has to wait for the best moment to run under the water.

Aims: developing imagination, vocabulary, sentence formation, reaction, auditory perception, auditory word discrimination

Materials: garden hosepipe (or watering can)

194 Secret messages

For this game you need several small balls (or hoops). A secret message is stuck to each ball. It could be a picture clue as to the whereabouts of the magic stones. For example, 'The magic stone is hidden behind the curtain'.

The adult rolls the ball away and one child has to point at the rolling ball until it stops. Then the child crawls to the ball with his eyes closed. Once he has reached the ball, he is allowed to look at the secret message.

The child then explains where to look for the magic stone. The group then looks for the magic stone together. Once it is found, then it is time for the next ball (or hoop).

Variation
The game can be varied by asking all of the children to close their eyes and indicate the course of the rolling ball with their hands, until it stops. Once the ball has stopped rolling the children open their eyes and check whether the direction indicated by their hands was correct. If anyone chose the right direction, they are allowed to read the 'secret message' on the ball, and so on.

Materials: stones, balls or hoops (you could also use wooden balls with a hole drilled through them, inside which the secret message could be hidden), paper for messages

The robber and the king

The robber has stolen lots of things from the king. However, the prince knows that, today, the robber is meeting up with his mate. This provides us with an opportunity to get the things back from the robber's hut (which could be made from a box, table, den made from gym mats, etc).

Everyone hides near the hut. The adult makes a continuous sound (using a triangle, bell, drum, etc). The children are only allowed to creep forward when the sound stops. This is the sign that the robber is far enough away for them to retrieve the stolen goods. The children quickly fetch from the hut as much as they can gather. However, as soon as the sound begins again, they have to get out of the hut and hide until the next time the sound stops. Once the children have managed to get everything out of the hut, they can take it back to the king. It is likely that a reward will be waiting there for them!

> **Materials:** a robber's hut (cushions, gym mats or furniture), an instrument to make a signal (triangle, bell or drum, etc), assortment of small objects

196 Where is the noise coming from?

A sound-making object such as an alarm clock, radio, tape recorder is hidden. Some jigsaw or inset puzzle pieces are laid out. When a child manages to find the noisy object, he is rolled inside a barrel to collect a puzzle piece. The puzzle piece could also be picked up with clothes pegs (good for developing fine motor skills and self-perception).

The puzzle should be selected to provide opportunities for practising a target sound: for example, a jigsaw puzzle with lots of pictures of objects beginning with the target sound, or a picture of a scenario that provides opportunities to practise a particular sentence pattern. The sound-making object is hidden again in a different place once the first child has selected a puzzle piece.

> **Materials:** barrel, jigsaw or inset puzzle pieces, a sound-making object such as an alarm clock, radio or tape recorder.

(197) Rolling ball

Some 'treasure' is hidden somewhere in the room. The adult rolls a ball. As long as this is rolling, the children are allowed to look for the treasure. However as soon as the ball stops they have to freeze and wait for the ball to start rolling again. (A small ball, or a big wooden bead, will roll for longer if it is rolled on the inside of a hoop.)

> **Materials:** ball or big wooden bead, hoop (optional), small objects to represent 'treasure'

(198) Dangerous journey

The journey to the magic castle is dangerous. Nevertheless everyone wants to get there, because the magician will tell a story to anyone who manages to get to the castle. The journey involves creeping along a marked-out path through the magic forest; the children have to stop immediately if they hear any sound – otherwise they have to go back to the start.

> **Materials:** chalk to mark out path

(199) Snake charming

The children pretend to be snakes by lying on the floor and closing their eyes. Then the adult finds somewhere in the room to sit down, and plays on a flute or recorder in order to charm the snakes. The children try to crawl and slither over to the flute player without opening their eyes.

Every time a child manages to find the right place, he is allowed to take something out of the flute player's basket, still with his eyes shut. He has to guess what he is holding in his hand. The basket contains a number of different items: for example, objects related to the target sound or objects that can be used for play afterwards, such as tea set items, things for a shop, models of zoo animals, and so on.

> **Materials:** flute or recorder, basket containing a selection of small objects such as a tea set, shop items, zoo animals etc.

200 Sound makers

Prepare a selection of different materials – dried peas, sand, crumpled tin foil, etc. Use these materials to create pairs of sound makers by filling two containers at a time with the same content. Empty film containers are particularly suitable – use a small spoon to fill them. Then the containers are held in the hand and shaken. We either look for identically sounding containers, or we try and guess the content of the containers.

> **Materials:** selection of materials, film containers or similar, teaspoons

201 Guessing sounds

The children take turns to lie on their tummies on a skateboard with their eyes closed. The adult has different sound makers in a basket and makes a sound until the child has reached her on his skateboard. Then the adult puts the sound maker back in the basket, and the child is allowed to open his eyes and say which sound maker was used to make the sound: 'You were using paper', or 'It was the triangle', and so on. The adult keeps changing their position in the room.

> **Materials:** basket, a selection of sound makers

(202) Hot word

One by one, each child sit on a swing and swings back and forth while the adult says different words. The child who is swinging has to immediately jump off the swing when he hears a particular word or a word beginning with the target sound. If he has listened and reacted correctly, he is allowed to thread a bead onto a string to make a chain. How long will the chain be?

Materials: swing, beads, string

(203) Back-to-back

We sit back-to-back with each child in turn. We tell a story and the child has to try and push the story-teller away every time he hears a previously agreed word or sound.

Materials: none

Listen carefully

Does a word begin with the target sound? The children take turns to lie in a hammock or on a platform swing with their eyes closed. The adult clearly articulates a series of words for the child who is swinging. The child lifts their hand every time they hear a word beginning with the chosen target sound. The adult puts a peg for a peg board into a basket every time the child has made a correct judgement. In the end, the child is allowed to put the pegs in the peg board to make a picture.

> **Materials:** hammock or swing, peg board and pegs

 Grab the right thing!

Children take turns to lie in a hammock or on their tummies across a platform swing. In a basket under the hammock there are different objects. The child's task is to fish out those things that begin with a particular sound. While doing this he names the item loudly and clearly.

> **Materials:** hammock or swing, basket, selection of small objects

206 Be careful!

Different claps demand different actions: for example, one clap means 'walk'; two claps mean 'stand', three claps mean 'sit down', and so on. The children have to translate acoustic signals into movements.

Materials: none

(207) Rhyming pairs

Rhyming pairs of items containing a target sound are put on the floor to the right and the left of each child. The children have to slide their fingers (initially alternating between left and right hand, later with both hands, or even both feet) to link the rhyming pairs. (To do this, they have to cross the midline, which facilitates the development of both halves of the brain.)

> **Materials:** selection of objects (picture cards can be used)

Variation
The children can accompany their actions with a magic spell such as: 'Hocus-pocus – cat to mat'; or 'Simsalabimbambum – ice to mice'; or 'Abracadabra – crown to town', and so on.

> **Materials for variation:** pairs of objects

Roll to the rhyme

Each child in turn is rolled backwards and forwards in a barrel between cards with rhyming words. The child who is being rolled picks up a card and is then rolled to the other words where he has to find the matching rhyming word. Again a magic spell can be said, as in the variation of Game 207, *Rhyming pairs* (page 256).

If a barrel is not available, the children can simply be rolled along in a stretched out position.

Materials: barrel, rhyming word cards

 Jump to the rhyme

Cards with rhyming words are spread out on the floor, so the children can jump from one to another. The adult throws the dice and the children jump the number of jumps indicated by the dice. Now they have to find a matching rhyming word and may either jump forwards or have to go backwards to the rhyming word. Who gets to the finish first?

Materials: dice, rhyming word cards

210 Boat or goat?

Play a minimal pairs rhyme lotto using predominantly sounds that the group has difficulties articulating. Because the words vary by one sound only, the children are forced to check their articulation, since otherwise they may be misunderstood. For example, if a child picks up the card with 'boat' and says 'goat', the person who has 'goat' on their lotto board will claim the card.

The lotto tiles could also be placed behind a 'mountain' made of gym mats. The players have to get behind the mountain to collect a card and travel back across the mountain. On top of the mountain they call out the word pictured on their tile and ask, 'Who has the lamb?' and so on.

Variation
The children could also have different things (real objects or picture cards) in front of them and ask where a particular object belongs: in a jar or in a car? In the tea or in the sea? On the table or in the stable?

Materials: lotto cards and board, gym mats (optional)

---

(211) Emperor, how far may I travel?

The children stand on the opposite side of the room from the adult and ask the adult, 'Emperor, how far may I travel?' Answers could involve first names, country names, towns, places and so on. The number of syllables in the answer determines how many steps the children are allowed to walk. For example, if the answer is Africa, the child is allowed to take three steps.

Materials: none

What is the shaker doing?

Everyone makes a shaker using empty yoghurt containers filled with different materials (for example, different grains, beans, small stones). Then the whole group recites a rhyme and moves according to the words, or everyone sings a song and moves to the tune while shaking the shaker. The following words could be used in a song:

We are walking around in a circle, circle, circle – you can't hear us, we don't make a sound – that's how we walk around in a circle.

We are taking small steps, small steps, small steps – and toddle in the middle – that's how we make small steps.

Now we are walking backwards, backwards, backwards – very high on tip toes – that's how we are walking backwards.

We are stamping like horses, like horses, like horses – the whole ground is shaking – that's because we're stamping like horses.

We are creeping like cats, like cats, like cats – on their soft paws – that's how we are creeping like cats.

We are sleeping like giants, like giants, like giants –
mh, mh, mh, mh, mh, mh, mh – but suddenly, but
suddenly – we have to sneeze – ah-ah-atchoo!

(Joecker D & Kleikamp, *1, 2, 3 im Sauseschritt. Lern-,*
Spiel- und Spasslieder, Menschenkinder Verlag, Münster)

Materials: clean, empty yoghurt containers,
materials for filling

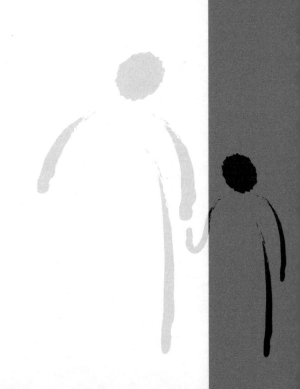

Spot, where are you?

The children play in pairs and both players are blindfold. One child pretends to be Spot the dog, and the other Spot's owner. The owner calls, 'Spot, where are you?' Spot barks or growls. The owner tries to find his dog. Spot, on the other hand, tries always to stay out of reach. Different variations are possible: for example, the cat mother may be looking for her kitten, and so on.

Materials: none

Part 4: Games for facilitating hand-eye coordination and finger motor skills

According to neurophysiological views, there are no specific dedicated speech centres within the brain. Instead there are intensive neurophysiological networks between speech, language and motor skills, particularly between speech and hand skills. The motor centres for speech, finger, foot and toe movements all partially overlap on the cerebral cortex. Therefore, by activating one area, neighbouring brain regions can also be activated. Daily finger exercises can therefore bring about considerable improvement in oro-motor skills.

Spider's web

Form a circle. One person takes a ball of wool, winds the string twice around their wrist, and says: 'My name is …', then throws the ball of wool to another child in the circle and asks, 'And what's your name?' In this way, one after the other, the children will be given the ball of wool and say their names. At the end, when everybody is linked by the ball of wool, they describe what it feels like to be connected with everybody else. Then they have to follow the line made by the wool back, in reverse order: the last player throws the ball of wool to the last but one player, while saying their name: 'Peter, catch the ball'. That person then has to roll up the piece of wool, check where it runs next, and throw it to the next person.

Aims: developing dexterity, hand-eye coordination, visual perception (following a line with the eyes), fine motor skills, consolidating children's names, sentence formation

Materials: ball of wool

215 What do you like doing?

Everybody gets into a circle. The leader takes a ball of wool, wraps the string around her waist once, while saying: 'I'm Maria and I enjoy walking!' Then she passes the ball of wool to the next child and asks, 'And who are you and what do you like to do?' This child also wraps the string around his middle once, says his name and what he enjoys doing, and then passes the ball of wool on to the next child. The game continues until everybody has had a turn. Everyone considers what it feels like to be connected by the wool.

Afterwards, the ball of wool goes back the way it came. The last player unwraps the last-but-one player, while saying: 'You are Julia and you like swimming', and so on. While doing this, the wool is wound onto the ball again.

Aims: developing dexterity, memory function, hand-eye control, fine motor skills, contact with others, gentleness, sentence formation

Materials: ball of wool

216 Who gets the clothes pegs?

Each child is given a clothes peg. All of the children spread out and find a place somewhere in the room. In the room, there are balls or other obstacles, which the children are not allowed to bump into. Then the adult says: 'Everybody put their clothes peg on Eve!' The children now have to run up to Eve without bumping into any of the obstacles, and peg their clothes pegs onto Eve's clothes. Then Eve calls out: 'Put all clothes pegs on …!' To do this, each child has to take a clothes peg off Eve's clothes and put it on to the named child.

Aims: developing room orientation, fine motor skills, gentleness, articulation of the consonant cluster *cl*, consolidating children's names

Materials: clothes pegs

(**217**) The hedgehog with clothes peg spikes

Cut out some hedgehogs from cardboard, using clothes pegs as spikes for the large hedgehogs, and paper-clips for the small ones. The hedgehogs provide opportunities to engage in role-plays: perhaps they meet, tell each other about their different adventures, become friends, look for food together, are scared of enemies, argue about the best place for hibernating in winter, and so on.

Aims: developing fine motor skills and finger agility, imagination, enjoying talking

Materials: cardboard, safety scissors, clothes pegs, paper-clips

(218) Long – longer – longest

The children thread acorns and/or horse chestnuts on to nylon threads to make chains. When they have finished, they compare their chains, laying them out next to each other and putting them into an order: which is the longest, which is the shortest and which ones are the same length?

Aims: developing finger motor skills, fine motor skills, understanding the terms long/short and their comparatives and superlatives

Materials: acorns and/or horse chestnuts, nylon thread, strong needles

(219) Throwing conkers

A large, empty egg box (or several smaller ones set close together) is placed on the floor. Some of the middle pockets are marked. These are targets to be aimed at, just as you would aim at a bullseye. Each child is given three or more conkers to throw at the target. The winner is the player who has the most hits. With older children, different pockets could have different scores, which the have to be added up at the end of the game.

The children could also try to gain an advantage by putting a spell on their conkers, so they land safely in the egg carton: 'Conker, conker, off the tree – in the egg box I want thee!', or 'Hocus-pocus witch's toe – in the egg box you will go!'

After several games, you can use the last game to tidy away the conkers: get the children to stand in a particular place and to throw the conkers into a box or basket.

Aims: developing hand-eye coordination, agility, consolidating the speech sound K, developing memory

Materials: large egg carton or a few smaller egg cartons, plenty of conkers

220 **Conker transformation**

Each child is given a piece of cardboard, colouring-in pens, glue and a conker. The child now has to glue down the conker and, by drawing around it, change it into an animal, tree, storybook character, or something similar. Each child explains what his conker has changed into and together everyone makes up a story featuring the transformed conkers.

Aims: developing fine motor skills, creativity, imagination, enjoying talking

---

Materials: cardboard, colouring-in pens, glue, conkers

Conker tricks

Using conkers, different finger skills can be practised:

◆ The conkers must be picked up with two fingertips only: for example, between thumb and index finger, index finger and middle finger, middle finger and ring finger, and so on.

◆ A conker is initially picked up using the index finger and the thumb, and is then passed to thumb and middle finger, thumb and ring finger, thumb and little finger, without touching the conker with the other hand or dropping it.

◆ A conker is placed in each gap between the fingers (thumb-index finger, index finger-middle finger, middle finger-ring finger, ring finger-little finger). Who can hold on to the conkers like this?

Aims: developing finger motor skills, ability to differentiate between different fingers, perceiving and naming individual fingers

Materials: conkers

Flood

This is a nice rainy weather story. First, sit the children down, one behind another, in a big circle.

◆ It is starting to rain. Use your fingers to imitate the rain. The first drops to fall are big drops, which you can imitate by drumming your fingertips on the floor, on your legs or arms, or on the back of the person in front of you, while articulating '*drip drop, drip drop …*'
◆ Soon the rain becomes heavier, and you have to move your fingertips more quickly, while saying, '*drip drop, drip drop …*', faster and faster.
◆ It is raining so hard now that you have to run for cover. (When the signal 'thunder' is given, each child has to jump up and find cover somewhere in the room.)
◆ In the end, there is a flood. Your way home has been flooded. Some stones (use beer mats, or squares of paper) are sticking out of the water. Balance on these stones to get home. Is anybody getting wet feet?

Aims: developing finger differentiation, body awareness, articulation of the consonant cluster *dr*, balance, body control

---

Materials: beer mats or squares of paper

---

(223) Windmills

Make yourselves some paper windmills and blow to get them moving. Who can get their windmill going, making the *sh* sound, so the wind can be heard? Afterwards everyone walks through the room (you could also go outside) with their windmill, so that it turns in the wind that their movement creates.

Aims: developing finger agility, fine motor skills, steering something in the air, articulating the *sh* sound

Materials: paper, sticks, nails

224 The kite's adventure

Everyone makes a paper kite. Then, using a needle, thread small pieces of plastic straw onto a piece of string to make the tail, or tie ribbons to the bottom of the kite. The children get their kites floating through the air by running with them when the 'wind' is blowing. The adult gives the sign for wind, for example, by raising her arms. When the adult lowers his arms, the kites have to come back down to the floor. Afterwards, the children sit down on the floor together and tell a puppet, or a reporter with a microphone, what their kites have seen and experienced.

Aims: developing fine motor skills and finger agility while making the kite, developing room orientation, visual perception, reaction, imagination, enjoying talking

---

Materials: paper, glue, pens, string, plastic straws, safety scissors, thread, needle, ribbons, puppet or 'microphone' (see Game 158, *Interview with a puppet*, page 210)

225 **Catching leaves**

Children are entranced by the idea of a storm in an autumn forest and fascinated to re-enact the way leaves might 'rain down' from the sky, as well as having great fun throwing them into the air. Collect a bag full of leaves to play the leaf-catching game. The adult or one of the children stands on a platform. The rest of the children recite the rhyme:

Autumn wind makes the leaves fly
Wants to catch them
Wants to get them from up high!

The adult or child on the platform drops a leaf or several leaves. The children have to try and catch the leaves before they hit the floor.

You could also collect particularly nice leaves, press them, then make imaginative pictures with them.

Aims: hand-eye coordination, developing articulation, memory

Materials: autumn leaves, paper, glue

226 I am getting dressed

Cut out pictures of clothing from catalogues. Then think about the order in which the clothes have to be put on. To do this, sit in a circle and place the pictures in the middle of the circle, in no particular order. One player starts by saying: 'I am putting on my pants and then …' At the same time, he throws a beanbag to another child. This child now continues with '… and then I put on my vest and then …', and throws the beanbag to another child.

The game becomes more difficult if each child has to repeat all of the previously named items of clothing, so that the sentence becomes longer and longer: 'I am putting on my pants, then my vest, then my socks and then …'

Aims: developing finger motor skills, recognising meaningful sequences, developing hand-eye coordination, sentence formation, articulation, memory

Materials: catalogue with pictures of clothing, safety scissors, beanbag

(227) Dressing dolls

Each child is given a paper doll and clothes to cut out. The clothes are cut out and placed on the doll in the correct order. While doing this, the children describe what they are doing: 'Now Peter puts on his trousers', or 'Sally puts on her tights'.

Aims: developing fine motor skills, articulation, sentence formation, practising personal pronouns *his/her*

> **Materials:** dolls and clothes made from paper/cardboard, safety scissors

(228) Making snow

Assemble a landscape, using a large piece of cardboard for a base, either using building blocks (which is more creative) or ready-made toys (toy houses, trees, benches, animals, figures). Then, by rubbing chalk across a fine mesh (eg, a sieve), make it snow across the landscape. While doing this, you can practise different sentence patterns such as: 'The … is white', or The snow is falling on the …', or 'It is snowing on the …'

When everything is white, carefully lift all the items off the baseboard until you are left with just an outline. Then turn the baseboard around several times and try to remember what has created the different shapes before trying to put the things back in the correct place again. Again, while doing this, different sentence patterns can be practised such as: 'The … was here', and so on.

Aims: developing imagination and creativity, dexterity, finger motor skills, sentence formation, articulation, visual perception – especially shape recognition

> **Materials:** cardboard as a base, building blocks or landscape toys, sieve, white chalk

229 Snowflakes

Use blue or black paper and white finger paint. The children take turns to dip their fingers in the paint and then let drops of paint 'snow' onto the paper. While saying a rhyme, they tap their fingers on the paper, following the speech rhythm of the rhyme: they could also let their index and middle fingers take it in turns to 'snow'. Here is a suggestion for a rhyme:

Tree, trar, trow: in winter there is snow.
Big flakes, small flakes, cold flakes, white flakes.
Tree, trar, trow: in winter there is snow.

The consonant cluster TR can be replaced with other target sounds.

Aims: developing finger motor skills, improving rhythm, developing articulation, memory training

Materials: dark paper, white fingerpaint

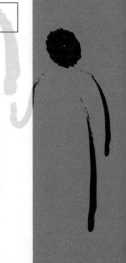

230 Freshly painted

Cut out pictures of toys from a catalogue. Ideally, stick them onto card so that they are more robust and easier to pick up. Now everyone pretends they are in a toy factory and all of these toys have just come off the production line. Because all the toys have just been painted, no one is allowed to touch them with their fingers. Instead, they have to pass them from person to person using clothes pegs.

The first child picks up a card, using a clothes peg, and calls out: 'Look out, here comes a freshly painted car!' He passes the card on and moves to the end of the conveyor belt. This means that the second child is now at the beginning of the line, takes a new card and calls out what is being passed along next. In the end, the toys get to the shop and the children can play shopkeepers.

Aims: developing fine motor skills, strengthening writing fingers, developing coordination, reaction, articulation, sentence formation

Materials: catalogue with pictures of toys, safety scissors, clothes pegs

(231) Balloon hockey

Each child is given a balloon and makes himself a bat by rolling up some newspaper. The bat has to be held with both hands like a hockey stick and the child has to try and shoot the balloon into a goal. An empty box, opening towards the child, is placed on the floor as a goal.

Before the game starts, a counting out rhyme is used to determine who is going first. You could also count the number of hits it takes to get the balloon into the goal. Here is a suggestion for the counting-out rhyme:

The bat for the balloon
Will be yours very soon.
Pick it up now, it's your turn.

Aims: developing articulation, memory, hand-eye coordination, encouraging children to cross the midline

Materials: balloons, newspaper, box for goal

(232) Clothes peg circus

Draw animals onto cardboard, cut them out and attach clothes pegs to represent their legs. In this way, the animals can stand up properly. A snake can be made by attaching one clothes peg to another. For crocodiles, the clothes pegs can be the body, to which a cardboard tail is attached. You will also need a cage for your wild animals: this can be made from a strip of cardboard to which clothes pegs are attached to make a fence. You could also cut out a circus director, a clown, acrobats, and so on. The arms of these figures can also be made from clothes pegs too.

Now everyone can start playing. First, the children discuss their programme – they need a circus director, an announcer for each act, an audience to applaud, and so on.

Aims: developing fine motor skills, strengthening writing fingers, developing imagination, enjoying talking

Materials: paper, cardboard, clothes pegs

(233) Fancy dress memory

Empty plastic yoghurt pots are placed upside-down on the floor. A string is attached to each yoghurt pot and a picture of a fancy dress is placed under each pot.

One child starts the memory game by picking up two pots by their strings and telling the others what pictures are underneath. If the pictures go together (eg, witch/broom, painter/paintbrush, wizard/wand), the child is allowed to take the cards away and put back the empty pots. If the cards do not go together, the pots are put back over the pictures and it is the next child's turn. Remember that the child is only allowed to hold the pots by their strings, and therefore has to lift and replace them carefully.

Variation
Vary the game by using it to practise the singular and plural of different nouns.

Aims: developing visual memory, hand-eye coordination, consolidating different sounds or words, vocabulary development

Materials: yoghurt pots, string, different pictures of objects

Wild or tame?

First of all, make symbols for 'tame' and 'wild' – they could, for example, be pictures of a growling lion and a dog wagging its tail. One child starts by picking up an animal card and trying to describe the animal. If another child guesses the animal, he is allowed to take the card to the correct symbol. If the animal is a wild animal, the child has to place the card inside a hoop made from corrugated cardboard, and stick plastic straws around the hoop through holes in the cardboard to create a cage. If the animal is a tame animal, the child takes the card and arranges a stable made from matchsticks around the animal.

Afterwards, you could play a memory game: 'Which wild or tame animal can you remember?' The child who remembers the animal is given the picture card.

Aims: symbolic understanding, describing animals, recognising and categorising common attributes, developing finger motor skills, memory

> **Materials:** paper/cardboard for the symbols, animal picture cards (perhaps from an animals pairs game), strips of corrugated cardboard, plastic straws, matchsticks

(235) Creepy-crawly

The children get together into pairs. One child lies comfortably on the floor, with his partner sitting next to him. The adult says the first part of a rhyme (see below), and the seated child has to guess the second part of it and use their fingers to represent a creepy-crawly which is crawling to the correct place on the child who is lying down. The index finger and the middle finger should alternate while crawling to a given body place. Then the roles are swapped.

Try using these rhymes:

◆ Creepy-crawly crummy – crawl to my [tummy].
◆ Creepy-crawly cringer – crawl to my [finger].
◆ Creepy-crawly croot – crawl to my [foot].
◆ Creepy-crawly creck – crawl to my [neck].
◆ Creepy-crawly cree – crawl to my [knee].
◆ Creepy-crawly cred – crawl to my [head].
◆ Creepy-crawly crin – crawl to my [chin].

Aims: developing auditory perception, contact with others, developing tactile awareness, finger motor skills, naming body parts, recognising body parts, vocabulary development, developing articulation (especially the consonant cluster CR)

Materials: none

(236) Magic beetle

Make a ladybird (or some other kind of beetle) from cardboard and attach a piece of metal to its 'stomach'. Then put a selection of objects on a table and make the beetle crawl to the different objects by moving a magnet underneath the table. The children take turns to describe where the beetle would like to crawl: 'The beetle is crawling to the fence', or 'The beetle would like to crawl to the fence', or 'Look out, the beetle is coming! It is crawling to the fence'.

Variation

You could also vary the game as follows. If there are enough small magnets for each child to use, you could take A4 pieces of cardboard and get the children to draw different 'stops' around the outside of their cardboard. Then the children make their beetles crawl in all of these different directions around the cardboard, talking about the adventures the beetles have on the way. A small magnet for each child and a paperclip underneath each beetle are sufficient for this variation of the game.

You could also use paper to fold a house for the beetle and then stick this onto the cardboard. In this way, the beetle can go to sleep in his house at the end of his journey. Maybe we can even hear him snore, *ch-ch*.

Aims: consolidating the sound B in a sentence, the consonant cluster CR, the sound *ch*, developing hand-eye coordination, imagination

Materials: cardboard beetle, small magnets, paperclips, glue, cardboard, colouring-in pens

(237) The hedgehog wakes up from hibernation

Cut out the body of a hedgehog from cardboard and attach clothes pegs for its spikes. While attaching the spikes, everyone closes their eyes. Did the children manage to get all spikes on the hedgehog's back, or did some end up on its tummy by mistake?

The hedgehogs go for a spring walk and talk about what they can smell, hear and see.

Why do hedgehogs have spikes anyway? It must be because the spikes are really sharp and help hedgehogs to fend off enemies. Hedgehogs are particularly scared of owls, for example. When an owl comes along, hedgehogs roll up into a ball and stick out their spikes. Now the children can play at helping the hedgehogs defend themselves. They take the spikes (clothes pegs) off the hedgehogs first, then a marble rolling inside a hoop (or a spinning top spinning) will represent an approaching owl. The children quickly have to re-attach the spikes to the hedgehogs. If they can manage to attach all the spikes before the marble or spinning top comes to a standstill, the hedgehogs are safe.

Afterwards, everyone searches the room for sharp or pointy objects. They cover the objects with a cloth and try to recall them from memory.

Aims: developing finger motor skills, tactile perception, imagination, auditory and visual perception, reaction, speed, practising the adjectives sharp/blunt, memory training

Materials: cardboard, safety scissors, clothes pegs, hoop and marble (or spinning top), pointy objects, cloth

(238) Shooting buttons

Tell the story of Mr Fat and Mr Thin. Mr Fat was so fat that, in the end, all the buttons burst off his jacket! The children are going to play with these buttons. First, they get together into pairs. Each pair is given two buttons, a piece of paper, a pencil and a large strip of cardboard, into which they have to cut three goals, each marked with numbers or symbols. One child begins by saying which goal he wants to hit. He then tries to shoot one button into the goal by holding the second button between his thumb and index finger and flicking it against the first button – just like the game Tiddlywinks. The number of shots needed to score a goal is recorded. A bonus point is given if the button has gone into the targeted goal first time. Before he starts shooting, each child says the following rhyme: 'A button, a button, a trouser button, another button that goes bang'. His partner listens carefully to ensure that the B really 'explodes'. Who needed the least shots?

At the end, everyone thinks about who or what is 'fat' or 'thin' – people, animals, lines, pens, trees, and so on. Maybe they can think of stories involving fat or thin people or things?

Aims: improving articulation of the speech sound B, finger motor skills, hand-eye coordination, developing imagination, practising adjectives *fat/thin*

Materials: buttons, paper, pencils, strips of cardboard, safety scissors

(239) Collecting honey

Each child makes a paper basket and places it in the 'beehive', which could simply be the table. To make their baskets, they all need their own square piece of paper, measuring 20–30cm each side. Fold up the baskets like this:

1 Mark the middle by folding once lengthwise and once diagonally and then unfold again. Fold the corners to the middle.

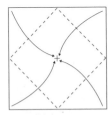

2 Fold the side edges to the middle and unfold again.

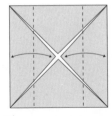

3 Fold the top and bottom edges to the middle and unfold again.

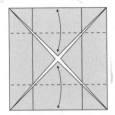

4 Fold two corners facing each other outwards.

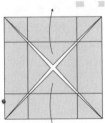

5 Fold up and down in the marked areas.

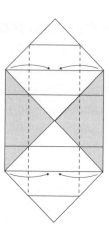

6 Fold the corners in the marked areas inwards.

7 Your box is finished!

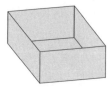

(Lucio R & Spütz J, 1997, *Verzaubertes Papier*; Don Bosco, München)

Now the children also need to make flowers, using coloured paper to fold or cut them out, and then spreading them around the whole room. Make little paper balls from tissue-paper, and put a little paper ball on each flower. Then all the children become bees and gather at the beehive, are given a plastic straw and fly off, one at a time. Each bee tells the others which flower it is flying to, for example: 'I'm going to fly to the red flower', makes flying arm movements, and flies to the flower with a buzzing *zzz* noise. Once at the flower it sucks up the pollen (the paper balls) with a plastic straw and brings it back to the beehive, where it puts the pollen into its basket. Then it is the next bee's turn to fly off.

This exercise can be made more difficult by putting out obstacles – then each bee has to find its own specific way and has to remember it, so it can fly back exactly the same way. The other children check whether the bee has remembered the correct way.

Aims: developing finger dexterity and agility, fine motor skills, articulation of the speech sound *zzz* and the consonant cluster FL, oro-motor skills, hand-eye coordination, practising holding on and letting go, room orientation

Materials: paper for folding, tissue paper, plastic straws, possibly some obstacles

(240) Waking up your fingers

All ten fingers are placed flat on the table. The children pretend that they are sleeping and want to wake them up, one at a time. In order to wake up a finger, they have to touch it. When a finger wakes up, it lifts and stretches up from the table, while the other fingers remain flat on the table. You can accompany this by calling out, for example, 'Right middle finger, get up!' Later, they can try to wake two fingers at the same time, for example, 'Right index finger and left little finger, wake up!'

Aims: developing finger motor skills, differentiating between different fingers, naming individual fingers, consolidating left/right awareness, developing articulation

Materials: none

Five fingers on my hand

Everybody finds a partner. They put one hand on the table or floor, say the following rhyme, and lift the corresponding finger, while the other fingers remain on the table or floor:

Five fingers on my hand, look after the animals in this land.
The thumb looks after the sheep – they say *bah*.
The index finger looks after the goats – they say *beh*.
The middle finger looks after the cows – they say *moo*.
The ring finger looks after the pigs – they say *oink*.
The little finger flits from here to there
And there to here,
And is not even scared of the wildest steer.

When saying the line about the little finger, the partners can tickle each other by nudging each other with their little fingers. At the end of the rhyme, the partners have to try to push each other away, forehead to forehead (like steers), until a red rag (or piece of paper) is shown and the steers move away from each other. The rhyme is similar to one created by Susanne Stöcklin-Meier, but the steer game was the idea of a child.

Aims: developing articulation, memory, differentiating between different fingers, naming individual fingers, developing body awareness, visual perception, reaction

Materials: red rag or piece of paper

(242) Thimble fight

Make some paper thimbles, which the children can colour in if they wish. Then the group gets together in pairs and starts the game with the thumb. Each child puts his thimble on his thumb. All his fingers are stretched out, but only the thumb with the thimble is greeting his partner's thumb by waving at it. The thumbs warm up by bending and stretching, and then they ask each other: 'Do you want to fight with me?' Now the partners try to knock off each other's thimble. The rule is that all the other fingers have to remain stretched out and are not allowed to help. When a thimble falls off, that child has lost. The next round starts and, this time, the thimbles are placed on index fingers. At the end, all the fingers will have had a turn.

To vary the game, you could change the rule: this time, all the fingers without a thimble have to make a fist – only the finger which has a thimble is stretched out.

Aims: differentiating between different fingers, finger dexterity and agility

Materials: paper, colouring-in pens, glue

(243) Finger puppet family

Make your own finger puppets – for example, a whole family with a father, a mother and three children – and get them to talk to each other. Alternatively, you could recite a rhyme such as:

This is the father, short and fat,
This is the mother in a new hat,
This is the brother wearing his cap,
This is the sister, a doll in her lap.
This is the youngest, baby child
And that makes up all of the family Wild.

Aims: developing finger dexterity and agility, imagination, enjoying talking, memory, differentiating between different fingers

Materials: paper, colouring-in pens, glue

(244) Play dough

Make your own play dough. To do this you will need: 1 cup of salt; 2 cups of flour; 2 tablespoons of vegetable oil; and enough water to mix the ingredients into a workable dough.

You can use the dough to make things for a pretend shop or zoo animals to accompany some of the other games in the book. Once you have shaped them, let them dry, paint them and play with them.

Aims: developing finger motor skills, imagination, enjoying talking

Materials: salt, flour, vegetable oil, water, cup, bowl, table cover

(245) A journey with the thumb tower and the index finger worm

One child begins the game and puts his fist on the table while stretching up his thumb and moving his fist in a circle. At the same time as he creates his 'thumb tower', the child sings the following words to any tune he likes: 'I am going on a journey, and who gets in? – Jacob in his brown jumper, he gets in'. Then Jacob has to hold the thumb of the first child with his fist. Now they both drive around in circles, and Jacob sings and decides, which child is allowed to get in next. The game continues until all of the hands have got in and, one at a time, have got off again: 'I am going on a journey and who gets off? – Eve with her blond hair, she gets off'.

You can vary the game by playing it with the index finger – what you have then created is an index finger worm!

Aims: developing tactile perception, body awareness, articulation, visual perception, coordination, fine motor skills

Materials: none

(246) Lid quiz

Containers of different sizes with screw-on lids are laid out, and then all of the lids are taken off and shuffled. One child has to select a lid with his eyes closed and then open his eyes to find and screw the lid onto the matching container, while saying something like: 'This lid goes with this jar', or 'I am screwing this lid onto this jar'.

Aims: developing visual perception, finger motor skills and finger dexterity, articulation

Materials: containers with screw-on lids

The catching fish

Make yourselves a 'catching fish', using two 14cm^2 sheets of paper for each child.

1 Fold both sheets diagonally, corner to corner, using your nail to run over the crease and fold out again.

2 Place the sheet of paper in front of you, so that a corner is pointing towards you. Fold the right, and then the left, corner towards the middle. Do the same with the second piece of paper.

3 You have created two pointy bags, which you now need to insert and glue into each other. To make the fish look more real, you can draw on eyes and cut out his mouth with fabric scissors (with a zigzag blade), in order to give the fish dangerous teeth.

4 Thread a bead on to a piece of wool (the older the children, the longer

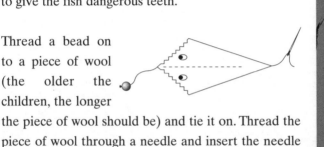

the piece of wool should be) and tie it on. Thread the piece of wool through a needle and insert the needle through the open mouth to the tail end, leaving about 1cm of string sticking out.

5 Fix the piece of string with tail fins. To do this, you need two tail fins: one tail fin is stuck on from the front, the other from the back. The end of the string has now been stuck between the two tail fins.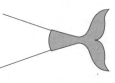

Idea from: Düsseldorfer E, 1996, *Das Neue Bastelbuch für Kinder*, bassermann, Niedernhausen, [p110]

Take the catching fish and push it gently so the mouth opens wide. While saying, 'Little catching fish, come and eat – eat whatever catching fish eat!' try and catch the 'food', ie, the bead.

Aims: developing hand-eye coordination, articulation of K and F

Materials: two pieces of paper per fish (14cm^2), pieces of wool, beads, needle, glue stick, thin card, safety scissors, pen

248 Bottle music

Put out different bottles and different coloured liquids (water, coloured with food colouring) in buckets or measuring containers. The children have to take it in turns to fill the bottles with water using a ladle and funnel. Each child has to say what he is filling the bottle with: 'I'm pouring lemonade [apple juice, a magic potion, blackcurrant juice, ink …] into this bottle!', and reinforce the sound of pouring with a *gl-gl-gl* sound. Once all the bottles have been filled up to different levels, the children can use a stick to hit the bottles and arrange them according to the sound that they make. In this way, the group can make some music together.

Aims: developing hand-eye coordination, articulation of B and GL, auditory differentiation, imagination

Materials: bottles, water, food colourings, funnel, ladle

(249) Shooting cans

Tin cans are used to build a pyramid. After a target rhyme (for example, 'Shrim, shram, shrown – kick the cans down!'), everyone tries to knock down as many cans as possible, using a ball. The child whose turn it is to shoot will rebuild the pyramid for the next child.

Aims: developing dexterity, body awareness, hand-eye coordination, articulation – the target rhyme can be changed, depending on what sound you would like to practise

Materials: tin cans, ball

(250) Is there something under the can?

Five cans are lined up in a row. The gap between the cans is so big that only one can be knocked over at a time. Each child in turn closes his eyes, while something is placed under three of the five cans. Then he opens his eye, shoots, and checks whether or not he can find something under the can he has knocked down. Items which could be placed under the tins include picture cards targeting a particular speech sound; individual pictures from a picture story which have to be sequenced at the end; picture cards from a particular category or word family for the children to act out – for example, from the word family 'walking', such as walking, limping, shuffling, jumping, marching, etc; or jigsaw puzzle pieces.

Aims: developing hand-eye coordination, articulation, vocabulary, imagination

Materials: tin cans, ball, picture cards or jigsaw pieces

Bubbles magic

One child recites a soap bubbles spell ('Hocus-pocus witch's doubles – make me lots and lots of bubbles'), to ensure the group gets lots of bubbles, and then he blows some bubbles. The others try to catch or pop the bubbles before they land on the floor.

Then another child tries to produce just one bubble, saying, 'Hocus-pocus witch's trouble – make me just one single bubble'). The other children follow the bubble with their eyes and clap their hands when the bubble bursts. The children could also follow the course of the bubble with their hands or arms, but without touching the bubble. Have everyone make a popping noise when the bubble bursts, articulating T or P or B.

Aims: developing gross motor skills, articulation, oro-motor skills, visual perception, concentration, consolidating the sounds T, P, B

Materials: bubble-making kit

(252) My mouth – a vacuum cleaner

Everybody makes themselves a supply of little paper balls – these represent dust. Use plastic straws to represent vacuum cleaners. Each child, if he throws a particular number or colour on a dice, uses his drinking straw to suck up a dust ball, holds his breath, and lets the ball fall into the bin. Who manages to clean up all their dust balls first?

Aims: developing fine motor skills, hand-eye coordination, oro-motor skills, coordination

Materials: paper, plastic straws, dice

Games for developing visual skills and hand-eye coordination

The following exercises aim to facilitate the development of observational skills and the ability to react in response to visual signals as well as hand-eye coordination.

253 Bubbles

The children watch a bubble move through the air and clap their hands when the bubble bursts. Before the adult blows the bubble, she says, 'Have a good flight, bubble!', or 'I am going to blow the bubble away!' in order to practise the consonant clusters FL and BL.

Materials: bubble-making kit

254 Musical magic

Several objects have been placed on the floor. Every object is covered with a cloth, which means it has a spell on it. The children walk through the room to music without touching any of the things on the floor. When the music stops, the spell is lifted and the children are allowed to guess the object nearest to them by feeling it through the cloth. Then they can lift the cloth to check whether they were right.

Materials: assorted objects, small pieces of cloth, music

(255) One, two, three – magic!

The magician shows the children how well he can do magic, holding up a tray with lots of different objects on it. Then he covers it with a cloth, says a magic spell, and makes one object disappear. The children then have to check under the cloth and guess which object has gone. (The number of objects is varied according to the age and developmental level of the group.)

Variations
The magician could add one thing instead of making one thing disappear. The children have to work out what is new on the tray.

The magician changes something about his appearance while concealed behind a cloth, and the children have to guess what has changed.

Materials: assorted objects, tray, cloth

256 Which shape is it?

The adult shows the children one shape at a time (a circle, cross, square, or triangle for example, drawn onto card) without being able to see the shape herself. The children have to copy the shape by drawing it into the air, once with their right hands, once with their left hands and then with both hands. The adult has to be able to guess the shape. Then the roles are swapped and one of the children shows the group a shape.

Materials: card

257 Mr Punch tells everyone where to go

Using tape, chalk, ropes, or string, mark out some routes and let the children walk along between these lines, following Mr Punch's instructions. If the route includes corners, curves and bends these terms can be worked on at the same time as directional language, such as forwards, backwards, right, left and straight on. In addition, the way of moving can be changed after each attempt (crawl, wriggle, walk on all fours, etc). At the end, Mr Punch shows us what he has found or discovered, or he tells everyone what happened to him at the place to which he has directed us.

> **Materials:** tape, chalk, ropes or string, 'Mr Punch' puppet

(258) Who can find the right way?

Several different routes marked out in ropes, chalk lines, or string all lead away from the same starting point. The children pick an item each from a 'feely' box, and have to put it with its matching picture card at the end of one of the routes. Because the routes cross, the children have to begin by working out the correct route, first following it from start to the finish with their eyes, and then balancing along the correct markers to the finish.

Materials: rope, chalk or string, 'feely' box, assorted items and matching cards

(259) Where does the journey end?

Get the children to use toy bricks to build a track and then drive cars along it. The destination of the cars is determined by drawing a picture card depicting different places such as a school, post office, department store, hairdressers, church, town, village, seaside, lake, mountain, restaurant, circus, playground, café, nursery, and so on. Each child picks a card and says, 'I am going to the …', or 'Will you come with me to the …', or 'Get in, I am going to the …' While driving, the child has to be careful always to stay on the road.

At the destination, there could be additional picture stories or situation pictures, so that the group can talk about what is happening there. A particularly funny or interesting story could also be told to Mr Punch (or Grandma, the princess, etc). The puppet could, for example, ask the children whether they have been to a particular place, and what happened there.

> **Materials:** toy bricks, toy cars, picture cards; puppet (optional)

(260) Where are we going?

Build a road using toy bricks, or draw it on brown parcel paper. There are lots of side streets coming off this road. At the end of each side street there is a picture card or a real object beginning with the target sound. The children pick a destination from a pile of cards and drive along the appropriate street to the object/picture in question.

Riding a motorbike would lend itself to practising BR or R words. Making *brrr* or *rrr* sounds the children could drive to the end of the relevant street where they find the object/picture card and then complete the word (for instance, 'br—*-ead*', 'r—*-ose*').

> **Materials:** toy bricks or brown paper, picture cards or assorted small objects, destination cards

261) Which vehicle is coming?

Build a road using toy bricks. The road has a zebra crossing for children (miniature toy people) to cross the road. The children guess different vehicles by touch from a 'feely' bag and warn the toy children: 'Careful, here comes a …' 'Careful, there is a … on the road!' 'A … is racing along!' Then they set off, but are not allowed to veer off the road.

You could also incorporate a traffic light, for which the group could say: 'Stop, stand still!' 'Red means stop!' 'Green means go!' The traffic light could be made by the children using thin paper and a torch. (They could also make a board, green on one side and red on the other; however, this would mean the children would not get an opportunity to use their fine motor skills to switch the torch on and off.) The traffic light or board is given to one child who then plays the role of a policeman.

Materials: toy bricks, toy people, 'feely' bag and assorted toy vehicles, thin paper and torch or red/green board for traffic light

262 The most beautiful necklace

Mr Punch would like to give the princess a necklace for her birthday. Unfortunately his fingers are not skilled enough to make one, and so he asks the children for help. Mr Punch has drawn an exact plan to show how he wants the necklace to look.

Draw a sequence of beads on a piece of paper, increasing the complexity of the necklace to increase the level of challenge in the game. You could alternate two (three, four) colours, or have two (three, four) beads of one colour at a time. While threading the beads, each child talks about what he is doing: 'A red bead, a blue bead …', or 'red beads, one, two, three; blue beads …'

Materials: Mr Punch puppet, paper and coloured pencils, assorted coloured beads, thread

(263) Who can take the journey without looking?

There are several obstacles in the room, all connected by a marked-out route. Lying on his tummy on the skateboard, each child has to follow this route. Then the child skates back to the starting point and tries to find the same way blindfold, or with eyes closed. If he manages it, he is given a card from a picture story. The process is repeated until the children have collected all the cards between them. Then everyone looks at the picture story together. Perhaps you can even re-enact it using role-play.

If no skateboard is available, the journey can also be made by crawling or walking on all fours.

Materials: obstacles (chairs, cushions, beanbags, etc), chalk, skateboard, picture story cards

264 Magic cloth

Four children hold a cloth by the corners, high above their heads, and let it flap gently up and down. Without touching this 'magic' cloth, the other children try to walk under it in order to collect something from the other side. For example, there could be some dolls waiting that are too scared to walk under the magic cloth on their own. If any child touches the cloth, he has to return empty-handed. Afterwards everyone plays with the dolls.

Materials: cloth, dolls or other objects (books, marbles, etc)

265 What does the clown like?

Make a clown's head with a big mouth and ask everyone to try to shoot a small ball through the mouth. Each time the children are about to throw the ball, they must ask the clown whether he likes a particular food. If the ball goes in his mouth it means that he likes the food; if the child who is throwing the ball misses, the clown does not like the food.

Materials: material for making clown's head, small balls

266 Who can remember everything?

A path is marked out to the magic castle. To the left and right of the path there are different objects. The children take turns to walk (or crawl or skip or jump) along the path. The castle door will only open if the child whose turn it is has remembered and can recall everything along the path (or half of the objects, or three objects – depending on the child's ability). Maybe the magician will show a magic trick as a reward.

Materials: chalk, assorted small objects

267 Handle with care!

Picture cards are spread out on the carpet. These picture cards have to be picked up with a clothes peg, named and then passed to another player, who also takes the card with a clothes peg and sorts it according to a particular system (for example, fruit, vegetables, etc). If a card drops to the floor, it has to stay there.

Materials: picture cards, clothes pegs

268 Penalty kick

Lotto tiles are spread face down in a goal area (which could be marked out by chalk lines, bean bags or cushions). Every player is given a lotto board. The players take turns to be in goal or to kick the ball. Whoever manages to shoot a goal is allowed to take a tile, name what it describes, and put it on the corresponding lotto board. Kicking the ball is done with alternate feet, first with the right and then with the left, or it can be batted with the hands (alternating the right and left hands). Before each kick, a command such as ''Simsalabimbambust – a goal is a must!', or 'Simsalabimbamboal – here comes a goal!' is recommended.

> **Materials:** lotto tiles and boards, material to mark out goal area

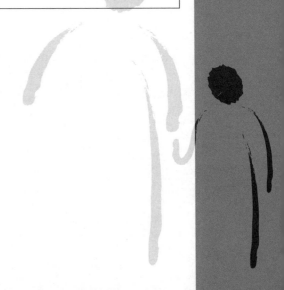

(269) Colourful birds

Colourful birds are made from folded paper, following the instructions below. Each child lets a bird fly, announcing, 'My bird is flying to the …!' or 'Fly quickly to the …, my little bird!' or 'Red (blue, yellow, green) bird, fly to the …!'

1 Crease the paper along the dotted lines, then fold in points 1 and 2. Fold down all of the upper part at the same time,

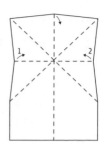

2 Fold both corners to the middle twice.

3 Crease along the dotted lines and then fold the wings out. Fold up the wing tips.

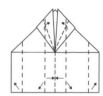

4 Cut out a swallow's tail and push it
into the swallow.

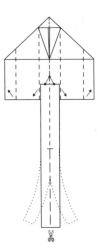

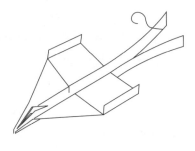

(1993, *Origami. Papierfalten leicht gemacht*, Proclama)

Materials: paper, safety scissors

270 Snap them up!

Each child in turn lies on his tummy across a hammock or platform swing and, while swinging, selects all the yellow beads from a selection in a box or tray on the ground. (Or red/blue/green beads; all round objects; all objects made of wood/plastic/paper; etc.)

> **Materials:** hammock or swing, box or tray containing an assortment of objects, some similar in type

271 Different balloons

A selection of balloons in different sizes and colours is lying on the floor. The children are asked to take, for example, all the big, red balloons to a specific place. To do this they have to walk on all fours and carefully push the balloons with their head. At the finish each child mimes an action and the others have to guess what it is. Actions could involve acting out different trades or professions – for example, pretending to be a doctor or a carpenter. Next, the small blue balloons need to be taken to the finish. These balloons could be transported by the children in a different way – for example, one child could balance them on his stretched-out hand, while another could walk with a balloon between his legs, or keep it in the air with a stick or a rolled-up newspaper.

> **Materials:** assorted balloons

272 Cat and mouse

Using a yoghurt pot, paper and some remnants of wool, have the children make an animal that is a predator. Then use corks as the animals which are hunted. The two types of animals could be a cat and a mouse, a fox and a hen, a stork and a frog, a frog and a fly, a snake and a mouse, and so on. Each cork is tied to a piece of string and moved by the children pulling the string. The children take turns trying to catch as many corks as possible using the yoghurt pot 'animal'. Before the start, the children could say:

Cat and mouse: 'Mouse, mouse, come out of your house!'
Fox and hen: 'Nin, nan, nen, now I want a hen!'
Stork and frog: 'Rog, rog, rog, the stork eats a frog!'

Snake and mouse: 'A giant snake is never late, and eats the mouse outside its house.'

Materials: yoghurt pot, paper, wool, cork, string

273 He who catches, wins

Balloons are filled with different things, such as stickers, small toys or sweets. Then, one at a time, let them drop to the floor from a chair or stepladder. The children have to try and catch the balloons before it touches the floor. If they manage it, the successful child is allowed to burst the balloon and see what is hidden inside. One could also use balls with pictures or messages.

> **Materials:** balloons, small items to go inside them

274 Closed bags

Different objects are hidden in little bags with different fasteners, such as ribbons, buttons, zips, poppers or hooks. The bags are lined up on the floor behind a line (use tape, ribbons or string). The children take turns to balance on this line and reach over to the bags, open a bag they have chosen, call out what is inside, and then close the bag again. The important thing is to have a large number of bags to provide the children with lots of opportunities for practising the different fasteners.

> **Materials:** selection of objects, small bags with different fastenings, tape, ribbon or string

275 Which fastener fits?

Provide a selection of bottles in different sizes, remove the lids, and jumble them up. The children have to find the right lid for each bottle and say 'This lid fits this bottle.'

> **Materials:** assorted different-sized bottles with lids

276 Quickly, quickly, wind it up!

Different objects have been hidden in the magic forest. The objects have been wrapped individually in boxes, and are attached to a piece of string, which reaches to the end of the magic forest. The end of the string is tied to a small wooden stick. The children can get the boxes out of the dangerous forest by winding up the string. However, they need to stop winding as soon as they see an agreed visual clue (for example, one of the children could shine a torch). While they are winding up the string, the children repeat the following rhyme until they have pulled the box to them: 'Quick, quick, quick, wind up the string, before the magician makes it go ping'.

> **Materials:** an assortment of objects, small boxes, string, stick, torch

Rocket ship

Each child squats down slightly and drums his hands on his thighs – that is the rocket launch ignition. In response to an agreed visual signal from the adult the children throw their arms up in the air and jump up, stretching out their legs. The children land on the moon, look through their binoculars down onto the Earth, and tell each other what they can see using Earth – Moon 'radio contact'.

Materials: none

 What a mess!

Everyone plays at shops, but there is a huge mess, because Mr Punch has been standing in for the sales person who has been off sick, and he has mixed up things on the shelves. The children have to recognise what is on the wrong shelf and then put it in the right place.

Materials: an assortment of items for playing 'shop'

(279) Dolls house

The group wants to play with the dolls house. The magician, who has conjured up some furniture to play with, is just leaving the house. Unfortunately he has conjured a lot of things into the wrong place: the cutlery is in the bathroom, the books are in the fridge, the bed is in the kitchen, the oven is in the bedroom, and so on. Everyone helps to tidy up the dolls house. While doing this, they are likely to have discussions, and to make or reject suggestions about what goes where. When they have finished tidying up, the children play together and could, for example, act out the daily routine of the doll family.

Materials: dolls house with dolls, dolls house furniture and accessories

Farm

Together everyone builds a stable and some paddocks by taking it in turns to place the toy bricks. While doing this, they could explain their choices to the group and influence the final result. Then the children decide what animals they want to buy at the auction. They also need food for each animal, which they could make out of play dough or modelling clay. Then they act out different farm scenarios.

Afterwards, can they list, without looking, all the animals, and do they still know off by heart what food was used? The animals are taken to the paddocks together. One animal has run away. Which animal is missing?

Materials: toy bricks, toy animals, play dough or modelling clay

Part 5: Games for promoting oro-motor function

Speaking, and particularly learning to speak, is a very complex process, demanding the ability to carry out specific movements of one's own volition. In addition, movements have to be sequenced in such a way that the sounds produced blend together to make a word. In his own brain, the child has to decide which word will follow which.

Precise and specific movements of the mouth, tongue and lips are necessary for good articulation. If a child has articulation difficulties, the cause may be a lack of mobility of the oro-facial musculature. That is why oro-motor exercises are necessary and helpful at the beginning of phonological therapy. These include:

◆ jaw exercises
◆ lip exercises
◆ tongue exercises
◆ blowing exercises

These exercises are particularly useful for increasing the child's awareness of his mouth, tongue and lips. The child learns to know and feel his mouth area. In addition, a general improvement of tongue and lip agility, coordination and movement skills, as well as a decrease of possible tension, is achieved, resulting in more relaxed oro-facial muscles.

Using a mirror can be a useful tool for many of these exercises. Each child can control his own movements using the mirror.

Jaw exercises

The following jaw exercises are for loosening up and decreasing tensions around the mouth.

(281) Fish babble

The room turns into the sea and the group become fish. Everyone walks through the room making swimming movements, and talks like fish: they move the lower jaw up and down, from side to side and backwards and forwards. The children visit each other, and tell each other stories in fish babble.

Variation
The group can also carry out this exercise by lying on their tummies on the floor, making swimming movements and talking like fish. The exercise is particularly effective if only the stomach touches the floor.

Materials: none

Lip exercises

Lip exercises facilitate lip seal (for example, in children who breathe through their mouths, and/or have developed incorrect swallowing patterns) and are particularly valuable when a child is unable to spread or push forward his lips.

(282) Where have my lips gone?

Put the bottom lip over the top lip to make it disappear, or the top lip over the bottom lip to make it disappear.

> **Materials:** none

(283) Monkey business

Everyone pretends to talk like monkeys by alternately pulling the lips to a wide grin and then pushing them forward while saying *eee* or *ooo* respectively.

> **Materials:** none

(284) Nimble lips

Two plates carrying different objects (counters, pens, toy cutlery, bottle lids, or edible items such as carrot sticks or apple slices), and two empty plates are prepared in readiness for this activity. Who can, using their lips, move all their objects onto the empty plate? Who finishes first?

> **Materials:** plates, a selection of objects

(285) Painting with obstacles

Who can paint and simultaneously hold a tongue scraper, a stick or a carrot slice between their lips? Obviously, the children's lips have to remain closed for this, which means that each one has to concentrate on holding and moving the paintbrush or pen, and, at the same time, keeping their lips closed while breathing through his nose.

> **Materials:** painting materials, small, safe items for holding in the mouth

(286) Lips dice game

Red, green, blue and yellow circles are drawn on a piece of paper, and the corresponding number of counters as well as a colour dice matching the colours of the circles, are put out. Depending on which colour is thrown, each child has to pick up a counter with his lips and put it in the matching circle.

> **Materials:** paper and colouring pens, coloured counters and dice

Popping cheeks

With their teeth together, the children blow up their cheeks. Each child's neighbour tries to 'pop' his cheeks from the outside.

Materials: none

 Horse and coachman

The children pair up as 'horses' and 'coachmen'. The coachmen drive the horses by means of skipping rope or ribbon reins. 'Gold' coins made from cardboard (prepared together with the children beforehand) are spread out on the floor. When a coachmen passes by a gold coin, he tries to get his horse to stop by saying 'whoa'. When all the gold coins have been picked up, try and make up a game using the coins, or role-play a fairy tale involving gold coins.

Materials: skipping ropes or ribbons, cardboard and gold-coloured paper for 'coins'

(289) Elephants

The group pretends to be elephants who have to carry logs from one place to another by holding plastic straws, pens, or similar objects between the upper lip and nose, or between lower lip and upper lip. The logs can then be loaded onto a train which runs on a track made from lined-up toy bricks.

> **Materials:** small items that can be safely carried in the mouth, toy train, toy bricks

(290) Popping champagne corks

The children find that their lips can pop beautifully – and they can use them to imitate champagne corks popping. (Empty) bottles are put out, corks are placed on the bottle openings, and the children use the sides of their hands to knock off one cork after the other while imitating the 'Pop!' of a champagne cork. To produce this noise, suck the lips between the teeth, and then open them forcefully to produce a loud popping sound.

> **Materials:** empty bottles, corks

(291) Candlelight

The children produce several *p* sounds, in quick succession, to make a candle flicker.

Materials: candle

(292) Pigs gallop

The group moves forward on all fours according to the number of moves indicated on a dice rolled previously, and push out their lips to make a grunting noise. The path to the pigsty is marked out with pieces of paper or newspaper. Who makes it to the sty first?

Materials: dice, paper

(293) Whistling

One person crawls around the room, blindfold or with their eyes closed, while the others warn of obstacles by whistling.

Materials: blindfold (optional)

Tongue exercises

Tongue exercises strengthen the tongue musculature, promote the development of the range and precision of movement and agility, as well as awareness of the inside of the mouth. The exercises will enable the children to be more able to carry out the tongue movements needed for speech articulation.

A child whose tongue is in the wrong position during swallowing will find it easier to work on a new swallowing pattern after having practised these exercises. Through this he will be able to learn how to swallow 'correctly', so that teeth or jaw misalignments can be prevented or corrected.

294 Busy bees

The group pretends to be bees who have to collect pollen. Paper flowers with round discs made from thin paper at their centre are spread out round the room or on the table. Everybody gets a little basket or plate and collects 'pollen' by using a plastic straw to suck up the paper discs.

> **Materials:** paper flowers and discs, plastic straws

295 Bears love honey

The group pretends to be bears who are eating their favourite 'honey' and are getting covered all over in the sticky stuff. They sit on the floor and realise that their hands (or feet or bottom) are stuck to the floor. They try to pull away their hands (feet, bottom), which is hard work. Only then do they discover that they have got honey all around their mouth and they try to use their tongues to clean themselves – top and bottom lip, nose tip, chin, right cheek and left cheek are all licked with the tip of the tongue. In the end, the bears have to have a shower. They push their lips forward and make a *sh* sound, to pretend water is running from an imaginary shower.

> **Materials:** none

(296) Spring clean

The group pretends that the inside of the mouth is a house. They have to give the house a good clean, because it is really dirty, due to the chimney sweep, robber or witch having dragged in a lot of dirt. The floor (the bottom of the mouth), the ceiling (the roof of the mouth), the walls (the inside of the cheeks) and the windows (the teeth) are particularly dirty. Therefore everything is cleaned thoroughly with a cloth (the tongue) – to do this, the tongue tip is moved back along the roof of the mouth, the tongue is rolled downwards to sweep the 'floor', the teeth are wiped at the top, bottom, inside and outside, and finally the inside of the cheeks is cleaned, too.

Materials: none

(297) Horse and rider

The children pair up as 'horses' and 'riders', using skipping rope or ribbon reins (see Game 288, *Horses and coachmen*, page 338). The rider clicks his tongue to get the horse to move. The same exercise could also be carried out with a home-made hobby-horse.

Materials: skipping ropes or ribbons, home-made hobby-horse (optional)

298 Fishing

Fish made from thin paper are moved from a big pond into a small pond by sucking them up with a plastic straw. Who manages to move the agreed number of fish or the most fish?

Materials: thin paper, plastic straw

299 Monkey mouth

Everyone pretends to be monkeys, jumping around and copying each other's movements. Of course, they also have to make a monkey mouth – the tongue is pushed behind the lower lip while lips are kept closed.

Materials: none

300 Cats

The children creep around like cats, arching their backs because someone is threatening them. Finally they slurp up some (imaginary) milk with their tongues by sticking out the tongue as far as it will go, and putting it back in again.

Materials: none

Parrots

The adult plays the trainer and the children pretend to be parrots. The trainer clicks his tongue, and the parrots copy him. The trainer holds a slice of carrot between his tongue tip and his upper lip – the parrots copy him. The trainer sticks out his tongue, moving it quickly from side to side or in and out between loosely closed lips and making different sounds – the parrots copy him.

Materials: carrot slices

 Cracker on the tongue

Who can balance a cracker (Twiglet, carrot slice, etc) on their stuck-out tongue, while walking carefully to an agreed destination? As a reward, the children are allowed to eat the item of food.

Materials: assorted small food items

Where am I allowed to climb?

Using his tongue, one child indicates to the others whether they should climb up or down. The other children take it in turns to stand on a stepladder or a rope ladder. If the tip of the first child's tongue is behind the upper front teeth, this means 'up', if the tongue tip is behind the lower front teeth, it means 'down'. You could also make a small ladder for a doll or Playmobil® figure to climb up and down.

Materials: ladder or rope ladder; small ladder, doll

Blowing exercises

Blowing exercises facilitate airstream production and control. They are particularly recommended for children who have difficulties with breath control and therefore lose air through the nose, into the cheeks or out of the mouth.

Bubbles game

One person blows bubbles, while another tries to catch and pop them.

> **Materials:** bubble-making kit

 Breath figures

Cut out small figures from thin paper. Using their breath, the children blow these figures onto the mirror or window.

Variation
Use a plastic straw to blow figures onto the mirror or window.

> **Materials:** thin paper, plastic straw

306 **Blowing feathers (1)**

Blow feathers through the air. Who can keep their feather up in the air the longest?

> **Materials:** lots of feathers

(307) Will you make it to the finish?

Specific targets are given, towards which each child has to blow a feather.

> **Materials:** lots of feathers

(308) Blowing goals

Use cotton wool balls or table tennis balls and try to blow them into goals.

> **Materials:** cotton wool balls, table tennis balls

(309) Labyrinth

A table tennis ball is blown along the paths of a labyrinth built with toy bricks until it reaches the exit. This exercise can be carried out using the mouth or a plastic straw.

> **Materials:** table tennis ball, toy bricks, plastic straw

(310) Let's make music

By directing their airstream into the top of a bottle, the children can produce different sounds. Through experimenting, each child will quickly work out that different bottles will produce different sounds. How about a little concert?

Materials: assortment of bottles

(311) Blowing up balloons

Everyone blows up balloons. The children play with them – and have lots of fun.

Materials: lots of balloons

(312) Paper bags

The children blow up paper bags and burst them.

Materials: paper bags

313 Wind instruments

The children try out different wind instruments, such as recorders, mouth organs, trumpets, and so on.

Materials: a selection of different wind instruments

314 Blow pictures

Wet blobs of water colour paint on paper are blown apart in different directions – this makes fantastic pictures!

Materials: paint, paper

315 Paper birds

Paper birds (see Game 269, *Colourful birds*, page 322) fly from one nest to the next. The nests can be marked out on a table, using, for example, chalk. To fly the birds, the children have to control how much air they let out in one breath. (Idea from: Franke U, 1993, *Artikulationstherapie bei Vorschulkindern*, Ernst Reinhardt Verlag, München.)

Materials: paper birds, chalk

(316) Paper ships

Home-made paper ships are blown from one side of the sea to the other in a tub filled with water.

Materials: paper ships, tub, water

(317) Blow pictures in the sand

Using a plastic straw, blow pictures onto fine sand.

Materials: fine sand, plastic straws

(318) Garage

A road is drawn on a large piece of brown paper, or built from toy bricks. At the end of the road is a garage which can be built from bricks, or made from a cardboard box. The children have to blow small, light, toy cars along the road into the garage, using a plastic straw.

Materials: brown paper, bricks, cardboard box, small toy cars, plastic straws

Part 6: Additional games for working on specific speech sound problems

Like the preceding oro-motor exercises, the following games also aim to involve the 'whole' child in order to provide him with as much foundation training for the brain as possible. The aim is for each child to have as many experiences as possible that facilitate and integrate his sense of balance, his self-perception and his sense of touch.

In order to be able to work on different problematic sounds with children it is necessary for the adult to be able to produce the target sound correctly. The adult also needs to be able to copy any child's incorrect representation of the sound by observing closely how the child produces that sound.

The games for working on S, SH and R sounds are grouped into two parts: 'Games for auditory discrimination' and 'Games for practising the target sound'. The aim is for the children to be able to tell the difference between the target sound and the wrong sound, using the auditory discrimination games. Once they are able to do this, you can move on to games for practising the target sound. If any child simply omits the target sound (for example, *un* instead of *sun*), you can immediately start with the games which practise the target sound. Some of the games can also be adapted for practising other sounds.

In all of the games which follow, the child-adult roles can be swapped once a child is able to produce the target sound himself (this usually happens very quickly when playing this type of game) so that sometimes it is not the child but the adult who discriminates between wrongly and correctly articulated sounds. By producing wrong and correct sounds alternately, discrimination is practised and consolidated.

Games for working on the S sound

AUDITORY DISCRIMINATION GAMES FOR THE S SOUND

If the sound is substituted by another speech sound, for example, F for S, so that a child says *fand* when they mean *sand*, or if a child sticks out his tongue between his teeth while articulating S, auditory discrimination games which focus on discriminating between the child's sound and the target sound have proved to be very successful. The aim is for the child to learn to differentiate acoustically, as well as visually, between the two sounds. Visual discrimination occurs by looking at mouth shape, acoustic discrimination by careful listening. At the same time, the child is likely to become more sensitive in his ability to perceive movements and touch (tactile-kinaesthetic differentiation).

Two countries (1)

The room is divided in two, so that there are two 'countries'. In one country, S is articulated correctly, in the other incorrectly. The adult now walks from one country to the other and talks in S-language with the (imaginary) people. The children have to decide whether or not the correct language is spoken in the corresponding country and use agreed signals: for example, when the wrong language is spoken, the children switch on a torch.

Materials: torch, if used

Bee or wasp

The adult pretends to be a bee or wasp. The bee produces a normal S, while the wasp gets it wrong. The children are bees and take turns to sit in the beehive (for example, in a box, under the table, behind a bench, in a tunnel made from gym mats, in the hammock, etc) – they only let in the bee, while the wasp is chased away and has to fly on.

Variation
The children lie on their backs with their eyes closed, and the adult pretends to be a bee or wasp, producing the correct or incorrect sound depending on which insect they are (see above). The children only respond to the correct S. When the bee arrives (you could use a cotton bud or something similar), it is allowed to land. To indicate this, the child whom the bee is visiting gives an agreed hand signal or some other indication, and then describes the place where the bee has landed. However, if a wasp comes flying along, the child signals that it is not allowed to land.

> **Materials:** box, gym mats, hammocks (if used), cotton bud or similar

(321) Snake visit

The adult pretends to be different kinds of snakes, or has a selection of wooden, paper or plastic snakes. The poisonous snakes hiss with the wrongly articulated S, the non-poisonous ones with the correct S. Each child pretends to be an animal of his own choice and only offers the non-poisonous snakes space in his cave when they come to him. The poisonous snakes are chased away.

Materials: selection of toy snakes, if used

Engine damage

A line is drawn across the middle of the floor, or running across a large sheet of brown paper, to symbolise a border. Then a road is drawn or built with bricks across the whole area. The road should have lots of bends and cross the border several times. At one side of the border, cars drive with the normally articulated S, on the other side, with the wrong S. The children take turns to push the car along the road while the adult makes the accompanying engine noise. Each child has to listen carefully to the engine noise and stop immediately when they hear the 'wrong' engine. Cars with the 'wrong' engines have to return to the start to be repaired and then they can have another go.

Materials: chalk, or brown paper

323 Hot or cold

An object is hidden somewhere in the room. Along the lines of 'hide-and-seek', a normally articulated S is used to indicate to the child who is seeking that he is getting closer and warmer, and a wrongly articulated S when he is getting colder and moving away from the hiding place.

Materials: none

324 How long can we make the chain?

If the adult says a correct S the children are allowed to thread a bead, or a ring, or even something edible. However, if the sound is wrong, the children have to wait.

Materials: beads or other items, thread

Button or counter?

There are two types of objects in the 'feely' box. Depending on the age of the child, objects can be of a similar kind such as, for example, buttons and counters, so that the child has to feel carefully in order to recognise the object, or easily distinguishable things such as nuts and bricks. If the sound has been articulated correctly, the child has to feel for a button, if the sound is articulated incorrectly, the child has to feel for a counter.

Materials: 'feely' box, selection of small objects

 Paper snakes

Cut out paper snakes together. Some of the snakes are marked with a dot – these snakes are poisonous and hiss with the wrong S sound. The other snakes are non-poisonous and hiss with the normally articulated S. The adult hides with the snakes and ensures that the child cannot see his lips while hissing. Then a snake starts to hiss and the child has to guess whether it is a poisonous or non-poisonous snake. The snake crawls out of his hiding place and the child can check whether he made the right decision by looking at the snake's marking.

Materials: paper, scissors, pens for marking

Games for practising the S sound

Once the children are able to discriminate between the correctly articulated S sound and the wrongly articulated S sound, you can use the following games to practise producing the normally articulated S.

Bees flight

Everyone pretends to be a bee and 'flies' through the room humming *sss* (tunefully). They fly from flower to flower and busily collect pollen with a plastic straw (see Game 294, *Busy bees*, page 342).

Materials: plastic straw

 Bee sting

One player pretends to be a bee and hums (tunefully) through the room, trying to sting the other players with the tip of his finger.

Materials: none

 The bee stings the thief

One child pretends to be a bee, humming *sss* and waiting by the beehive at the other end of a tunnel made of gym mats or tables. The other players want to steal some honey and crawl through the tunnel to the beehive. The bee tries to sting the thieves with his fingertip as soon as they come out of the tunnel.

Materials: gym mats or tables

Paper aeroplanes

Everyone folds paper aeroplanes and aims them to land on an area marked out on the floor as an airfield. If the aeroplanes are started from a place higher up – for example, a rope ladder, climbing bars, a table, an armchair, the stairs – it can be even more fun. While the aeroplane is in the air, everyone makes an *sss* sound.

Materials: paper, rope ladder etc (as above)

 Hissing snakes

The group pretends to be snakes and slithers through the room making a hissing noise *sss* – possibly for as long as a visual signal is visible.

Materials: none

 Rope snakes

Take some long pieces of rope, pretend they are snakes, and snake them along the floor while making an *sss* sound.

Materials: long pieces of rope

333 Snake race

Lay out some coloured pieces of A4 paper or coloured building bricks with the colours matching the colours on a colour dice. Depending on what colour the children throw, they are allowed to snake along to the piece of paper/brick of that colour, while hissing a correct S sound. Each child then curls up next to the correct piece of paper and waits for his next turn.

Materials: coloured paper or bricks, a colour dice

334 Talking with the animals

Game 333, *Snake race*, can also played with fabric, paper, rubber, plastic or wooden snakes. A course is marked out using coloured toy bricks, the colour dice is thrown and, according to the colour, the snake moves forward with a hissing *sss*. Other animals are lined up next to the coloured markers along which the snake is moving. Now the snake can talk to the animal next to the brick he has landed on in S-language.

Materials: toy snakes, toy bricks, colour dice

Catch game

The children work in pairs and a yoghurt tub is made into a snake, while a cork becomes a mouse. The snake hisses *sss*, and wants to catch the mouse. The cork-mouse is attached to a piece of string, which can be pulled while the other player tries to catch the cork with the yoghurt tub.

Materials: yoghurt tub, cork, string

 Run and catch game

The children work in pairs and one player pretends to be the snake and hisses *sss*, while the other player pretends to be the mouse. Once the snake has caught the mouse, the roles are swapped.

Materials: none

(337) The snake frightens the magpie

The children pretend to be snakes by hissing a properly articulated *sss* and then they lie curled up in the hammock, on the floor or in a hiding place. A magpie (perhaps a hand puppet) has stolen the princess's jewellery (real costume jewellery, or pictures cut from a catalogue). The bird flies over the snake, is startled every time the snake hisses, and then drops a piece of jewellery because it is frightened. The jewellery is then returned to the princess. Perhaps the princess will offer a swap: a piece of jewellery for a pretzel, which could be threaded onto a piece of string.

Materials: hammock, magpie puppet, jewellery items, pretzel

(338) Bursting balloons

Lots of balloons are drawn onto a sheet of brown paper. Everyone pretends to blow up the balloons by making a noise. Then they try and hit the balloons with a little spear. When we hit a balloon air escapes with a fine *sss* sound.

With little stickers (or plasters) the children can repair the balloons and blow them up again. This way, every balloon can be hit several times and repairing the balloon with small stickers is fun and, in addition, makes high demands on the child's finger (fine motor) skills.

Materials: paper, coloured pencils, stickers

Games for working on the SH sound

AUDITORY DISCRIMINATION GAMES FOR THE SH SOUND

If the children are articulating this sound incorrectly, initial auditory discrimination games are useful to teach the child to tell the difference between the correct and the incorrect sound, both visually and acoustically, as well as through increased awareness of corresponding oro-motor movements and sensations inside the mouth.

Two countries (2)

The room is divided into two countries. In one country, trains drive with the correctly formed SH; in the other, with the incorrectly formed SH (the children's current representations of this sound). The adult pretends to be the trains, for example, by swinging a long ribbon to represent the wheel of the train. The children, in their turn, pretend to be the driver and give the signals. The train is only allowed to drive on when the correct SH sound is produced.

Materials: ribbon

 Locomotive damage

Each child in turn pretends to be the train. A ribbon swung with his arm represents the wheel. The child 'drives' through the room as long as the adult produces a correct SH sound. If the adult says the wrong SH, the train has to stop immediately to be repaired.

Materials: ribbon

341 Toy train

The group lays down a train track using toy bricks or building blocks. Then each child runs a toy train along the track. However, the train is only allowed to run if the adult is making the correct SH sound, otherwise the train has to stop immediately.

Materials: toy bricks or building blocks, toy train

342 Can you make it to the treasure?

Each child is given two A4 sheets of paper and uses these sheets to move forward to get to the finish line. The adult pretends to produce gusts of wind by saying SH. If the adult produces the correct SH, the children may take the sheet of paper from behind them, place it in front of them, and take a step forward. However, if the gust of wind is produced with the wrong SH sound, the sheet is not blown forward and they are not allowed to move the piece of paper – instead they have to wait for the next gust of wind.

Materials: two A4 sheets of paper

(343) The wind is blowing us away

The children are standing with both feet firmly on the floor. If the wind (the adult) blows with the correct SH, it blows up one of the children's legs so that each child is standing on one leg only. If the adult blows the wrong SH, they are allowed to put their legs back down again. Then it is the other leg's turn. The same game can be played using the arms. The children could also be asked to close their eyes during play.

Materials: none

(344) Flying cloth

The adult and each child in turn swing a cloth together. As long as the adult is producing the correct SH, the wind blows and the cloth flies freely through the air. If the wrong SH is produced, the child has to quickly stop so that the cloth crashes down.

Materials: cloth

Palm tree in the wind

A home-made palm tree, with leaves made from strips of paper or tin foil, can be shaken or blown as long as the wind is blowing – that is, as long as the correct SH sound is being produced by the adult.

Materials: paper or foil for 'palm tree'

Ribbon in the wind

The children make a ribbon fly as long as long as the wind is blowing – that is, as long as the correct SH sound is being produced by the adult.

Materials: ribbon

Games for practising the SH sound

Once the children can all discriminate between the correct and wrong representation of SH, the following exercises can be used to practise the correct articulation of SH.

347 Across mountains and through valleys

The adult and the children pretend to be trains. Ribbons waved with the right arm represent the wheels, and a second ribbon that two people hold with the left hand represents the buffer. The group starts by driving around the room together, making the correct SH sound. You can drive over mountains (made from gym mats) and through tunnels (made from gym mats, tables and chairs). Perhaps everyone could end up in a magic forest, in which a magician puts a spell on the train so that it now makes a different sound when it runs. For example, the magician might say, 'Simsalabimbamboo – now the train says "shoo, shoo, shoo"!' Different syllables can be practised in this way.

> **Materials:** ribbons, gym mats, tables, chairs

348 Buying tracks

Each child buys tracks from the adult. Every piece of track costs a proper SH, or a syllable containing a proper SH. Once the whole line is complete, the train is allowed to run, making a SH, SH, SH sound as it goes along. Every time it stops at the station, people get on and off, or something is loaded into the carriages.

> **Materials:** none

349 We pretend to be the wind

The group pretends to be the wind and, with an SH sound, blows different things (feathers, paper balls, ping pong balls, etc) off the table, from their hands, into goals or towards different finishing lines.

> **Materials:** assorted light objects that can be blown

350 Sailing ships

With an SH sound, everyone blows home-made sailing ships (for example, made from paper, bark or nut shells) across a bowl, from one side to the other.

> **Materials:** home-made sailing ships, bowl, water

351 Windmills (2)

Everyone waves scarves or ribbons and accompanies their actions with an SH sound. The adult is the main windmill which determines the rhythm. The other windmills are linked to the main windmill and copy its actions.

> **Materials:** scarves or ribbons

(352) Waving a cloth

The group holds a big cloth by the edges and makes a SH sound to represent the wind which keeps the cloth moving – quietly at first, with gentle up and down movements, then louder, and correspondingly more forcefully.

Materials: big cloth

(353) Flowing ribbons

Making a SH sound, everyone waves a ribbon. How many rhythms (fast, slow, smooth, jerky) and patterns (up, down, in spirals) can the children find?

Materials: assorted ribbons

(354) Blowing feathers (2)

The group tries to keep a feather blowing in the air while making a SH sound. Alternatively, they could blow the feather towards a specific goal, still making the SH sound. While doing this they can say, 'I am blowing the feather to the box. SH …!'

Materials: feathers, box or other goal (optional)

355 Putting out candles

Everyone very carefully tries to blow out a candle, making an SH sound.

Materials: candles

356 Flying objects

The children let home-made paper aeroplanes or birds, feathers or balloons fly down from up high and, at the same time, make an SH sound until the flying object has landed. The SH represents the wind, which makes the things fly.

Materials: paper aeroplanes, birds, feathers, balloons

Blowing down trees

We blow over home-made paper trees with a SH sound. Who manages to blow down the most trees using the sound 'SH'?

Variant
A dice is thrown and the children are allowed to blow over the number of trees indicated by the dice.

> **Materials:** paper trees, dice (optional)

 House of cards

All together, or in pairs, the group builds a house of cards, which is then blown over by the children making a SH sound.

> **Materials:** playing cards

(359) Large cloth

Several children hold a large cloth by the edges. One child pretends to be the wind and makes lots of SH sounds. Then he crawls underneath the cloth, while the others follow his 'SH' sounds and wave the cloth accordingly – gently for softer sounds, more rapidly for louder.

Materials: large cloth

(360) Is there a storm brewing?

Each child in turn lies on his tummy on a skateboard, which could, for example, represent a surfboard and, as soon as the wind blows (in other words, the child produces a strong SH sound) he is rolled through the room by the others.

Materials: skateboard

A sailing boat rocks across the water (1)

The children take turns to lie on their tummy across a big exercise ball, which represents a sailing boat. The children pretend to be the wind by producing a SH sound and, if the wind is strong enough, the adult will keep the sailing boat moving by rocking the ball backwards and forwards.

Materials: big exercise ball

 A sailing boat rocks across the water (2)

The children lie in a hammock or sit on a swing, which represents a sailing boat. They pretend to be the wind by producing the SH sound and, at the same time, the adult pushes the hammock or swing rhythmically backwards and forwards.

Materials: hammock or swing

(363) Water jet

The children use their arms, or even their entire bodies, to impersonate the rising and falling jets of a water fountain. The movement of the water fountain involves an SH sound which becomes louder as the water rises and softer as it falls.

Materials: none

Games for working on the R sound

Before beginning to work on the production of this sound, auditory discrimination games (exercises) may be necessary. This will enable the children to learn to differentiate visually and acoustically between the correctly formed R and their own incorrect production of the sound. They will also become more aware of the motor movements involved in saying this sound.

AUDITORY DISCRIMINATION GAMES FOR THE R SOUND
At this more advanced level, the games for auditory discrimination can be carried out with the roles reversed. This time the child produces the sound, and the adult decides whether the sound has been produced correctly or incorrectly.

364 Two countries (3)

The room is divided up into two countries. A road which repeatedly crosses both countries is marked out on the floor using chalk or bricks. In one country, cars drive with a normal R sound; in the other, with the R sound produced by the children who experience difficulty with this sound. The adult represents a racing car, using the different R sounds, and each child in turn can pretend to be a policeman who will disqualify the racing car if it drives with the wrong engine in either of the countries. Then the children are put in charge of the racing car, and they have to stop when the adult produces the wrong engine sound for the country the car is in.

Materials: chalk or bricks

Racing cars

A racetrack is marked out on the floor or on a large sheet of brown paper using chalk or bricks. The adult drives the racing car as in Game 364, *Two countries (3)*, and is disqualified by the children as soon as she drives with the wrong engine – that is, incorrectly formed R sound). Then the children take it in turns to drive the racing car while the adult continues to imitate an engine R sound. They have to stop immediately if the engine is not working properly.

Materials: brown paper, chalk, bricks

 Is the crane broken?

The children pretend to wind up their arms or legs using a crane. If the adult produces a correct R sound, accompanied by a winding action, the children, depending on what has been agreed, lift a leg or an arm if they are standing – they could lift their tummies, heads, or bottoms if they are lying on their backs or fronts. However, if the adult produces the wrong R sound, the crane will not work!

Materials: none

(367) Is the handle broken?

A toy vehicle is tied to a piece of string, which in turn is tied to a reel. If the adult produces the correct R sound, the vehicle can be reeled in. If the wrong R is produced, the handle is broken and so the children have to stop reeling in the vehicle.

Once the children are all able to discriminate between the correct R and the wrong R sound, the following exercises can be used to practise producing the correct R sound.

> **Materials:** toy vehicle, string, reel

Games for practising the R sound

Rolling objects

The children roll different objects (balls, hoops, rolls, etc) and accompany their actions by saying *rrr*.

> **Materials:** objects to roll – balls, hoops, etc

 Can we hit the goal?

The group tries to roll different objects into a goal (or even several goals), which can be drawn in chalk or marked out by toy bricks, beanbags, etc, and accompanies the objects on their way by saying *rrr*.

> **Materials:** objects to roll, objects to mark out goal

What is the traffic light saying?

The children build roads with toy bricks, or draw them in chalk on the floor, or on large sheets of brown paper. They then drive toy cars or motorbikes along the roads while saying *rrr*. On the roads, there are also traffic lights (for example, made by the children from cardboard and thin red and green paper, then lit up using a torch – see Game 261, *Which vehicle is coming?*, page 316). The child whose turn it is has to keep an eye on the traffic lights and, of course, stop at red.

Materials: toy bricks or chalk, toy cars or motorbikes, cardboard, red and green paper, torch

 Rocket

The child sits on a swing and imagines himself flying a rocket while the adult turns him round and round, winding up the ropes of the swing. Then the adult lets go of the ropes, and the swing rapidly twirls round and round, unwinding – the rocket is landing! The child has to produce an R sound until the swivel movement of the swing has stopped. The game can be played with eyes open or closed.

Materials: swing

Rolling skateboard

The children take it in turn to lie on the skateboard and, as soon as each one produces an R sound, the adult pushes the board in order to make it *rrr*roll.

Materials: skateboard

First to the finish?

Everybody has a toy vehicle which has been attached to a reel with a long piece of string (see Game 367, *Is the handle broken?*, page 386). The vehicles have to be raced to the finish by everybody reeling in their string to make their vehicles move. The reeling-in actions are accompanied by saying *rrr*.

Materials: toy vehicles, string, reels

Ball in a hoop

A ball is rolled along the inside of a hoop. As long as it is moving, everyone makes an R sound and follows the movement with their eyes.

Materials: ball, hoop

375 Rolling hoop

Each child rolls a hoop and, as long as it is rolling, accompanies the movement with the sound *rrr*.

Materials: hoops

376 Theft

The robber has stolen something from Mr Punch: this could be (home-made) gold coins (see Game 288, *Horse and coachman*, page 338), pictures that the children have previously painted, or beads and rings which the children have made from play dough or clay, threaded onto a piece of string and given to Mr Punch as a present.

The robber is not afraid of anything apart from fierce wild dogs. The children pretend to be ferocious dogs and frighten the robber with their dangerous growl (*rrr* or *krrr*). In fright, the robber drops one of the items he has stolen. One of the dogs picks it up and returns it to Mr Punch. Mr Punch continues to send all of the dogs until he has recovered all his stolen items.

Materials: Mr Punch puppet, coins, pictures, beads etc (as above)

Brrr!

The children pair up as horse and rider, using ribbons for reins. They ride to different marked-out places to collect treasure (any assortment of toys or small objects) that has previously been hidden there. However, the horse will only stop and let the rider collect the treasure if the rider pulls on the reins gently and at the same time says a proper *brrr*.

> **Materials:** ribbons, assorted small objects for 'treasure'

(378) Crow feed

All the children are crows. Different objects are hidden under a cloth, including about ten identical things that the crows will like to eat – for example, wooden beads or nuts. The crows hunt for the objects under the cloth. Everyone is delighted when they feel a piece of food – they shout *krrr* or *krar* (*kre, kree, kro*), then flap away to put it safely in the nest (on a table, or in a corner).

Variant
The game becomes even more varied if the nest can be attached somewhere higher up, so that the children have to climb there using a rope ladder, a stepladder or a box.

> **Materials:** beads, nuts, etc to represent crow food; box or bowl for nest; rope ladder, stepladder or box (optional)

Games for working on the F sound

(379) Missile

The children throw a beanbag with a long tail (for example, a ribbon attached to the beanbag) to each other. While throwing, they imitate the sound of this 'missile', using an *fff* sound.

Materials: beanbag with ribbons attached

(380) Burst balloons (1)

Several 'balloons' cut out from paper are attached to a pin board. The children throw child-friendly darts to hit the balloons. Every time they hit a balloon, they can imitate the escaping air with an *fff* sound.

Variation
The children could try and burst the balloons without looking, using a pencil. Ask the children to stand directly in front of the pin board, close their eyes and poke holes in the paper balloons using a sharpened coloured pencil or a little wooden skewer. Every time a child hits a balloon the air escapes, making an *fff* sound.

Materials: cut-out paper balloons, pin board, child-friendly darts, sharpened pencil or wooden skewer (optional)

(381) Burst tyre

The children take it in turn to drive along in a car (sitting on a skateboard being pushed or pulled by the adult), keeping their eyes closed. Every time the child feels that he has driven over a 'nail' (some kind of small obstacle, eg a stick or small toy brick previously placed on the floor), he imitates air escaping from a tyre with an *fff* sound.

Variation

If no skateboard is available, the children can also be pulled along on a blanket. The wooden sticks slow down the movement, which means each child will be able to feel them.

> **Materials:** skateboard or blanket, sticks or small toy bricks

Spray can

Picture cards with simple symbols or drawings such as a triangle, a square, a circle, a tree, or a house are spread out, face down in front of the group. Each child picks up a card, looks at it, and then puts it back again, face down. Then he draws the picture in the air, making it as big as possible, moving his whole arm as if he is using an imaginary spray can – he starts spraying with an *fff* sound. The other children have to guess what the drawing is supposed to be. Then the roles are swapped.

The symbols or pictures could also be made from sandpaper and be guessed through touch, before they are sprayed into the air.

Materials: picture cards

 What did you spray?

The children could also take turns to 'spray' the pictures from Game 382, *Spray can,* onto each other's backs. To do this, get them to use their fists or fingers to firmly paint on the backs of their neighbours and produce an *fff* sound as they work. Their neighbour has to guess what their partner has 'sprayed' on their back.

Materials: picture cards

Games for working on the D and T sounds

384 Boxing (1)

Pretend to make boxing movements, accompanied by D or T sounds. Boxing movements are stronger for the voiceless T than the voiced D.

> **Materials:** none

385 Raindrops

Roll out play dough into a square on the floor. Tap the play dough using the fingertips and accompany the actions with D or T sounds. These raindrops will leave many indentations.

Variation
Raindrops can also be played with the toes, rather than the fingers. This can be made easier by putting the play dough against the wall and sitting on the floor.

> **Materials:** play dough

(386) Pressing out puzzle pieces

Press out the pieces of a new puzzle from the back of a baseboard, and say D or T while pressing them out. Use a different fingertip for each puzzle piece. Afterwards, sort the puzzle pieces back onto the baseboard.

> **Materials:** puzzle

(387) Target board

Attach a target to the wall, and get the children to dip their fingertips in finger-paint and to try to hit the middle of the board without looking. They should accompany their actions with a D or T sound.

> **Materials:** target, finger paint

(388) Burst balloons (2)

The group cuts out balloons from coloured paper and pins them onto a pin board or puts them on the carpet. Using a coloured pencil, try to 'burst' the balloons and imitate the bursting sound by saying T.

> **Materials:** cut-out paper balloons, pin board, sharpened pencils

389 Finger play

Tap as many objects as possible around the room, and accompany your taps with a D or T. The children could also tap each object five times, using all five fingers.

Materials: none

390 It's raining

Everyone dips their fingers into blue finger paint and, one at a time, places their fingers onto a piece of paper. This creates lots of raindrops, whose noise the children can reinforce with D or T.

Materials: paper, blue finger paint

391 Dripping tap

Draw a tap on a piece of paper, with a container underneath. The tap regularly drips into the container. Just as in Game 390, *It's raining*, encourage the children to use their paint-covered fingertips to create 'raindrops' and imitate them falling steadily with D or T.

Materials: paper, blue finger paint

(392) Tapping balloons

Try to keep some balloons up in the air, using only the fingertips to tap them briefly, while saying T. Later on, you could also say, *tap tap*.

Materials: balloons

(393) Tap!

Put some small items (beads, pebbles, toy bricks, etc) out on a tray. While one child covers their eyes, a particular item is chosen. Then the child who has had their eyes covered is allowed to look again and take items from the tray until he reaches for the item previously selected. When that happens, everyone calls out *tap!*, and another child takes a turn.

Materials: tray, selection of small items

(394) Tip-top-tap!

Some of the children close their eyes and the others touch them in three different places saying, with each touch, *tip – top – tap!* The children who have had their eyes closed have to indicate the last touched area or even all three. Then the roles are reversed.

Materials: none

(395) No through road

Use folded cardboard to build rows of houses, which will have passages running through them. The children are given small toy cars and have to try to drive through these passages. However, if one of the passages is blocked by a parked car, the child has to blow his horn with a *doot doot* or a *toot toot*. This alerts the owner of the car who comes to move his vehicle.

(Idea from, Baumgartner S, 1992, *Sprachtherapie mit Kindern*, Ernst Reinhardt Verlag, München.)

Materials: cardboard, toy cars

(396) Will the tunnel open? (2)

Build a tunnel from gym mats, or alternatively use a table as a tunnel. Each child in turn lies on a skateboard, which represents a vehicle with a horn. The tunnel is closed and will only open if the horn is pressed and produces a loud *toot toot* sound (see also Game 395, *No through road*). The horn could have had a spell put on it by a magician, so that when it blows, it blows out different syllables such as *ta-ta, te-te, too-too, tow-tow, ti-ti, toi-toi* – but only one sound will open the tunnel.

Behind the tunnel awaits something to be loaded, or perhaps the child who has opened the tunnel is allowed to claim and eat a salt pretzel hanging on a piece of string using only their mouth to catch it.

If the skateboard is supposed to be a tractor, the child drives around with a *tack, tack, tack* or *tuck, tuck, tuck*.

Materials: gym mats or table, skateboard, objects to be loaded, pretzel, string (optional)

Games for working on the CH sound

(397) Woodcutters

Working in pairs, each child holds one end of a ribbon, which represents a saw. They pretend to be woodcutters and make sawing movements. Every time they saw down a tree, they make a CH sound.

Variant

If the exercise is too difficult with the ribbon (holding it taut can be tricky), you could also use a stick with a paper saw blade on it – the children can make this themselves from a large sheet of heavy paper.

> **Materials:** ribbons, stick with paper saw blade (optional)

(398) Dog and cat

Everyone pretends to be either a dog or a cat. The children could even make some paper masks to wear. If the dog gets too close to the cat, it arches its back and hisses at the dog, *chchch*! Hand puppets are also well suited to this game.

> **Materials:** none; optionally, paper dog and cat masks, or hand puppets

Cat mother

Each child makes himself a cat mask, puts it on, and has to pretend to be a cat mother protecting its young (you could also use a little basket with pictures of kittens or soft toy cats). Every time the nosy adult tries to sneak up too closely to the basket, the cat hisses, *chchch*. Role reversal is possible. The mask could also be made in such a way that the children can not see anything, and have to listen carefully for the approaching adult.

> **Materials:** paper cat masks, basket with cat pictures (optional)

 The witch and the animals

The witch in this game does not like animals. That is why the animals are hiding in the forest (they are hidden around the room). The witch looks for the animals and chuckles, *chchch*, every time she finds an animal. She locks the animals in a cage (made from bricks or cardboard strips, with pegs as a fence). It follows that a rescue mission has to be thought out. Can Mr Punch or the magician help?

> **Materials:** bricks or cardboard, pegs

Games for working on the G sound

If the sound G is replaced in spontaneous speech by D, the children can use their fingers to push down the tip of the tongue against the floor of the mouth when they are supposed to articulate a G.

Heel walk

Everyone walks on their heels to an agreed finish, and accompanies the walk with the sound *ggg*. They could also walk on their toes and say *ttt*, or everyone could alternate between *ggg* and *ttt*.

> **Materials:** none

 Horse riding

The children sit on stools, or backwards on chairs (to represent a horse), and swing their arms. When they swing up, everyone makes a D sound; when they swing back, they make a G sound. Then they rock backwards and forwards with the upper body and head, and say D and G respectively. Then they move their heads down, forwards and back up, accompanying the movement with D and G.

> **Materials:** stools or chairs

Juice tasting

Lay the table for a juice tasting – glasses are filled with imaginary juice and the group makes an accompanying pouring sound, *ggg*. Then the children taste the juice and describe what it tastes like (sweet, sour, boring, yummy, good, delicious, refreshing etc). Continue to pour new juices into the glasses and to make the *ggg* sound while pouring.

Materials: drinking glasses

Geese cackle

Fold geese from paper and let them swim in the bathtub. The geese talk to each other, *ga, ga, ga, ga*. The goose mother calls her goose children *gagaga, gegege* or *gigigi*.

Materials: craft paper for folding

405 Fox and hen

The hen cackles nervously, *gagaga*, when it discovers the fox, and runs away with an excited cackle. Most of the time, the hen is able to save itself from the fox by making it back to its little run.

Variation
Pretend a yoghurt tub is the fox, and a little cardboard disc on a piece of string is a hen. The fox tries to 'catch' the hen when the yoghurt tub is put over the small cardboard disc. The hen runs away with a scared *gagaga* – using the string, it can be pulled away quickly.

> **Materials:** none; yoghurt tub, cardboard disc, string for variant

Games for working on the K sound

If a child normally replaces K with T, he can use his finger to push down the tip of his tongue to the floor of his mouth when he is supposed to say a K.

Boxing (2)

Use a ball hanging in the air as a punch bag. Every hit is accompanied by a K sound. You could also pretend to shadow-box, and reinforce it with K.

Materials: ball, string

Hammer and nail

Everyone hammers imaginary nails into a workbench using a toy hammer or their fists, and accompanies the hammering with lots of Ks.

Materials: toy hammers

Chopping wood

Chop imaginary wood using an imaginary axe and accompany the work with K.

Materials: none

Popping bubbles

The children lie on the floor and pop imaginary bubbles blown into the air by the adult. To do this, each child lies on his back, stretches out his arms sideways at a right angle, and makes an *rrr* sound. When a bubble drifts past, the child shoots up his arms and says K, while clapping his hands together.

Materials: none

Can you catch the fly?

The children lie on their backs, arms stretched out to the side, and say *rrr* – they lie in wait for flies and mosquitoes. When they discover an (imaginary) mosquito, they shoot up their arms and say K, while clapping their hands together.

Variation
The children lie on their backs on the floor, stretch their arms out sideways at a right angle, and make an *rrr* sound. The adult dangles a fly, or some other creature, made from paper or cardboard, on a piece of string above the upper body of each child. The children have to try to catch the creature by shooting up both stretched arms and changing the R to a K. The piece of string must only be pulled straight up or lowered down, and not moved sideways.

Materials: none; paper 'fly', string for variant

411 The crow

The children lie on their backs in a hammock or on the floor and try to scare the crow flying above (a hand puppet or bird folded from paper) by making a K sound. Out of fright, the crow drops a stolen coin it is holding in its beak every time a child claps his hands. When the children have collected all the coins, they return them to Mr Punch. Mr Punch is likely to have some sort of reward ready, such as a little salt pretzel to thread on a piece of string for every coin returned to him.

(Idea from Franke U, 1993, *Artikulationstherapie bei Vorschulkindern*, Ernst Reinhardt Verlag, München.)

Materials: crow puppet, paper coins, Mr Punch puppet, pretzels

Games for working on the P and B sounds

Exploding lips

Bits of paper are torn from a sheet of paper and individually placed on a child's closed lips. While doing this, the child should tilt his head backwards. Then encourage the children to make an explosive P or B sound with their lips and blow away the pieces of paper.

Materials: none

 Lip smacking

Everyone smacks their lips. To do this, the lips are pressed between the teeth and then opened suddenly with some pressure.

Materials: none

 Blowing out candles

Everyone tries to blow out a candle with a big, voiceless P. The cheeks should not be puffed out to do this.

Materials: candle